MONEY TALKS
and SO CAN WE

Also by Ron Blue
Generous Living

MONEY TALKS
and SO CAN WE

How Couples Can
Communicate About:

- Spending and Giving
- Getting Out of Debt
- Investing
- Planning for Retirement
- And Other Money Matters

RON & JUDY BLUE

with Jodie Berndt

ZondervanPublishingHouse

Grand Rapids, Michigan

A Division of HarperCollinsPublishers

*To the Principals and Staff at RBC who model this way of living
on a daily basis. You are a great encouragement to us.*

Money Talks and So Can We
Copyright © 1999 by Ronald W. and Judy Blue

Requests for information should be addressed to:

ZondervanPublishingHouse
Grand Rapids, Michigan 49530

Library of Congress Cataloging-in-Publication Data

Blue, Ron, 1942–
    Money talks and so can we: how couples can communicate about spending and giving,
getting out of debt, investing, planning for retirement, and other money matters / Ron
and Judy Blue with Jodie Berndt.
       p.   cm.
    ISBN 0-310-22461-6 (hardcover). — ISBN 0-310-22266-4 (softcover)
    1. Married people — Finance, Personal. 2. Interpersonal communication. I. Blue,
Judy, 1944– . II. Berndt, Jodie, 1962– . III. Title.
HG179.B5653   1998
332.024'0655—DC21   98-39128
                                                       CIP

Hardcover editions are printed on acid-free paper and meets the American National
Standards Institute Z39.48 standard.

Interior design by Sherri Hoffman

Printed in the United States of America

99 00 01 02 03 04 /❖ DC/ 10 9 8 7 6 5 4 3 2 1

CONTENTS

10.04

97699

Part One

Bridging the Financial Communication Gap

Chapter One

Making a Statement

The Purpose of Money and Marriage

I looked at the calendar, mentally counting the months until our second child would be born. 1968. It was a new year, marked in our lives by Ron's new job, a new home in a new city, and the impending arrival of a new baby. No wonder we felt unsettled.

Not that Ron really noticed. Immersed in his work with a national accounting firm, he was gone each week from Sunday until Friday. We figured we'd be in for some changes when we moved from New York City to Dallas, Texas—but neither of us had anticipated how much Ron would have to travel, or what his schedule would mean for our relationship.

Of course, I wasn't complaining. Ron earned a good living and provided well for our family. I couldn't wait until the baby arrived! We already had a daughter—Cynthia—and I liked nothing more than to take her to the park and watch her play with the other toddlers whose mothers had become my friends and support system in Ron's absence. Surely another baby would double my joy, bringing with it an increased sense of purpose and fulfillment as I threw myself into motherhood.

Yet something was missing, and I knew it. Ron had a passion for his career, and I wanted more than anything to be supportive. After all, I knew several women who were in the same boat, women whose husbands worked long hours in jobs that often kept them away from home. Who was I to find fault with our circumstances?

I looked at the calendar again. Cynthia wouldn't see her daddy for another three days. That couldn't be helped, of course. But I wish I had had some idea—some warning—of how our lives would change when Ron accepted this new job. I wish we had counted the cost . . .

—Judy Blue, Dallas, 1968

Judy and I have been married for more than thirty years. I've spent most of that time as a professional financial advisor, serving as a consultant to some of the wealthiest individuals and corporations in America. I've written books about money, conducted seminars about money, and told thousands of people how to better manage their money. But when it comes to actually talking about money—*our* money—with Judy, the challenge takes on a whole new dimension.

I have the financial credentials to write this book, and Judy and I have spent several years studying and teaching courses that deal with marriage relationships. But perhaps our best qualification for presenting this information is experience: in three decades of marriage, we have made just about every financial mistake you can think of. We've bought houses we shouldn't have, invested for the wrong reasons, and listened to faulty financial counsel when we wanted to rationalize our poor decisions.

But even more than these things, our biggest financial frustrations stem from a basic difference in the way Judy and I view money. In a nutshell, she is a saver, while I am a spender. Judy is not cheap, but she never wants to spend more than she has to. I, on the other hand, grew up in a family where we wore only hand-me-downs, played with broken toys, and had barely enough money to buy food. To me, spending money is a symbol of comfort and achievement. When Judy and I look at our budget, I figure it's a guideline for how much we ought to spend, and I feel good when we spend it all. Judy, meanwhile, likes to make a game of seeing how much we could have left over at the end of the month!

But before we go any further, I want to point out that while much of this book is written using the pronoun "I," the material we will include is actually a compilation of our shared thoughts and experiences. Rather than dividing the book into a series of "Ron" and "Judy" articles, we have written each chapter together, editing and revising the information with both of our perspectives (different as they often are!) in mind. Being a more frequent speaker and author, I (Ron) got the job of narrating our stories and the lessons we have learned.

No matter how similar or different your financial perspectives are, talking to your spouse about money is rarely easy. In fact, statistics show that half of all marriages end in divorce—with the majority of these citing "money problems" as the number-one factor in the breakup. But in reality, *there is no such thing as a money problem*. What looks like money trouble in a marriage is almost always symptomatic of something else: a distorted view of money, a lack of understanding about the true purpose for marriage, or a basic inability to integrate the two and communicate effectively with your spouse about finances.

There is no such thing as a money problem.

If you had known Judy and me when we lived in Dallas, I doubt you would have been able to detect her unspoken frustrations or my preoccupation with my career. More likely, you would have seen how well I provided for my family and applauded the attention Judy lavished on our children. Our human desire to care for our loved ones—which often fuels the drive for wealth accumulation—is a natural and even noble impulse. But is there more to the picture?

When you think about things like success, personal fulfillment, and satisfaction, how important is material wealth in the equation? Be honest with yourself. If you're like Judy and me, you may wrestle with the lines that distinguish material wealth from life's true riches: personal freedom, fulfillment, and joy. Whether consciously or subconsciously, many of us have accepted the cultural view that says money buys opportunity which equals freedom and independence which means success which translates into happiness, fulfillment, and satisfaction. Economic security, therefore, becomes a necessary prerequisite to every other goal.

And what happens when that economic security is threatened? What if your wife spends too much? What if your husband makes a risky investment—and it flops? What if you face a debt overload … or financially meddlesome in-laws … or an economically uncertain future? Before you start lashing out or clamming up or feeling down or stalking off or scheming about ways to find more money to throw at the problem, stop and take a look at money and your marriage within the bigger picture.

Do you know what money really is? Do you know what it's for, and how to use it? And what about marriage? Do you know why you got married in the first place? Was it for shared intimacy? Companionship? Love? Understanding the purpose behind money and marriage serves as the basis for everything this book has to offer, from learning how to communicate with your spouse to making financial decisions that will enrich your marriage and your life.

THE PURPOSE OF MONEY

Money is not, as popular culture might assert, a measure of personal success, self-worth, or satisfaction. Having money—or *more* money— is not even a guarantee of security or financial freedom: I've talked to too many anxious, uptight rich people and too many secure, contented poor people to fall into the trap of thinking that money can buy peace of mind.

Many spiritually minded people are reluctant to discuss or associate themselves with financial matters. Yet Jesus Christ talked about money more than anything else!

So what is money, and what is it for? Many spiritually minded people are reluctant to discuss or associate themselves with financial matters, thinking (perhaps) that such an affiliation might imply greed or a worldly preoccupation with wealth. Yet Jesus Christ talked about money more than anything else! Scripture contains more than 2,300 references to money and possessions, repeatedly underscoring things like money's temporal value, noting—to paraphrase verses like Psalm 49:17 and 1 Timothy 6:7—that "you can't take it with you."[1] God doesn't associate money with any lasting accomplishments or standards of achievement. Instead, the Bible points to money as a tool, a test, and a testimony.

Money Is a Tool

Scripture tells us in Job 41:11 that everything belongs to God. And, as King David put it in 1 Chronicles 29:14, everything we have comes from God's hand. Therefore, since our money ultimately belongs to God, every spending decision we make has spiritual implications. It doesn't matter whether we buy a bigger home, pay for sports camps and piano lessons, or make a financial contribution to our church or another charitable organization. All we are really doing is using money to accomplish or achieve a broader objective. Money is a tool.

As you consider your spending habits and priorities, ask yourself this question: *Am I using my money—my tool—the way God wants me to?*

Money Is a Test

In Luke 16:10–11, Jesus tells his disciples that "whoever can be trusted with very little can also be trusted with much, and whoever is dishonest with very little will also be dishonest with much. So if you have not been trustworthy in handling worldly wealth, who will trust you with true riches?" How we handle money, then, is a test of our faithfulness. Far more than a question of statistics or numbers, our financial management style reveals our true priorities. And as Jesus goes on to say, "No servant can serve two masters. Either he will hate the one and love the other, or he will be devoted to the one and despise the other. You cannot serve both God and Money."

To apply this principle in your daily life, look at your checkbook register, your tax return, and even your weekly schedule. Do you pass the test? Ask yourself, *Am I serving God or money?*

Money Is a Testimony

Matthew 5:13–16 points to our responsibility to be "salt" and "light" to those around us, letting our light shine so that "they may see your good deeds and praise your Father in heaven." Our spending habits are a direct reflection of our values and beliefs, and the way we use money sends a message to the world. People can see, at least to some extent, how we spend our money: it is evident in such things as the homes we live in, the entertainment we choose, the cars we drive, the clothes we wear, and the hobbies we pursue.

With this in mind, the questions we must ask ourselves include: *Do my spending or giving habits bring glory to God? Can people tell that I am a Christian? Do I look different from the world?*

How are you using the tool God has given you? Does God have your allegiance—or are you more attentive to your job, your income, and the things that money can buy? If your spiritual testimony were recorded based on a peek inside your checkbook, your closet, or your garage, what would people know about you? More importantly, what would they know about God?

The point is not how much or how little you have; it's how you perceive and handle the resources God gives you. I want to point out that none of the principles we'll cover in this book are intended to convey or support an "anti-wealth" message. Being or getting rich is not a sin. In fact, the Bible even offers a strategy for accumulating wealth: "He who gathers money little by little makes it grow" (Proverbs 13:11). The point is not how much or how little you have; it's how you perceive and handle the resources God gives you.

Likewise, your perspective on marriage can make all the difference to your effectiveness as a couple. Just as you can have money without fully realizing its benefits and uses, you can also be married without appropriating all that God offers via the relationship. The key to unlocking your full potential begins with recognizing God's purpose for marriage.

THE PURPOSE OF MARRIAGE

When Judy and I were first married, neither of us were Christians. We didn't know what the Bible had to say about marriage, or what God might want for our relationship. All we knew was that we were committed to our marriage. Our parents had been committed to their marriages, and we figured we could make things work just as well, if not better, than they had.

What we failed to realize was that God didn't want us to be committed to our marriage; he wanted us to be committed to each other. We had fallen into a legalistic, self-righteous trap common to many couples, including Christians: We said that divorce was not an option—yet we did very little to nurture our relationship and each other. I was committed to making my business grow, Judy was committed to our children, and together, we were committed to preserving the institution of our marriage. Plowing our parallel rows, we experienced very little conflict, and therefore, we figured, we had a relatively "good" marriage.

Looking back, I realize how far short we fell. Things like cherishing, protecting, and honoring one another were not part of our everyday vocabulary; they weren't even our long-term goals. It was only after Judy and I became Christians that we began to discover the biblical design for marriage, with its emphasis on the importance of mutual love and respect. The more we read it, the more we realized that the Bible was a great "how to" book on marriage. Once we changed our focus from being committed to our marriage to being committed to each other, we were able to appreciate and appropriate God's plan for our relationship.

One of the most basic purposes for marriage is *procreation*. Starting with Adam and Eve, God gives us the responsibility to "be fruitful and increase in number" (Genesis 1:28). Pursuant to this charge is the task of raising our children; as Proverbs 22:6 puts it, "Train a child in the way he should go, and when he is old he will not turn from it." In other words, God gives us marriage as a vehicle for having and raising children.

Another biblical purpose of marriage is to *promote God's kingdom*. Ephesians 5:23–33 reveals how the marriage union reflects Christ's relationship with the church. Husbands are called to love their wives, caring for them as thoroughly and selflessly as Christ cared for us when he gave his life so that we could be made holy. Wives are to respect their husbands even as the church acknowledges Christ's lordship. This kind of love and respect includes patience, kindness, loyalty, and a host of other virtues.

In the financial realm, this loving, respectful relationship enables husbands and wives to communicate freely about budgets, investments, spending habits, and the like. And in a broader sense, by representing Christ and the church, our marriages showcase God's love to our neighbors, our coworkers, our friends, and our family.

Finally, the marriage relationship allows us to *provide* for one another physically, emotionally, and intellectually. God created Eve as a helper for Adam, a partner who would complete him. Likewise, in 1 Timothy 5:8, God calls a man to provide for his wife and family, a role which includes everything from financial caretaking to serving as a spiritual and emotional "umbrella" in their lives.

These roles—procreation, promoting God's kingdom, and provision—are just three of the many purposes God has for marriage. They are not meant to be an exhaustive list; rather, you can use them as a springboard for discussion as you discover God's specific purpose for your marriage. If you would like to know more about what the Bible says about marriage and our roles as husbands and wives, contact Family Life Today. A subsidiary of Campus Crusade for Christ, Family Life Today offers conferences and other materials designed to enrich your marriage and family relationships. You may write to the ministry at 3900 N. Rodney Parham; Little Rock, Arkansas; 72212. The telephone number is (501) 223–8663.

DEVELOPING A PURPOSE STATEMENT FOR YOUR MARRIAGE

Once you are armed with an understanding of money and the purposes for marriage, you can use this information to develop your own personal mission or purpose statement. Your purpose statement encompasses the character traits, goals, and achievements you want to pursue. It helps define how you use your resources, including your money and your time. And since every marriage is unique, your purpose statement will reflect your individual priorities, values, and goals based on the specific things that God has called you to be and to do.

Steven Covey, author of the best-selling *The Seven Habits of Highly Effective People*, likens a personal mission statement to the United States Constitution, which serves as the standard by which every law in the country is evaluated. With a mission statement, Covey says, you have "the vision and the values which direct your life. You have the basic direction from which you set your long- and short-term goals. You have the power of a written constitution based on correct principles, against which every decision concerning the most effective use of your time, your talents, and your energies can be effectively measured."[2]

Not long ago, our church sponsored a business luncheon. I attended, along with dozens of men and women I recognized as intelligent, successful CEOs and other corporate leaders. Partway through the seminar, the speaker asked how many of us had a mission statement for our organizations. Almost every hand in the place went up. Next, the speaker wanted to know how many of us had an individual purpose statement that we could apply to our own lives. Again, most of the group responded affirmatively. Watching the faces around me, I raised my hand to interrupt. "How many of you," I wondered aloud, "have a similar purpose statement for your marriage or your family?"

No one did.

I was amazed. All around me were men and women who had achieved all manner of success, who had intentionally set and pursued specific goals for their businesses and their personal lives. Yet not one of them had applied a similar strategy to their marriages. In fact, none of them had even considered the idea—yet when they stopped to think about it, they found themselves intrigued by the prospect.

Writing a purpose statement—whether it's for a company, an individual, or a marriage—is not something you do overnight. When a friend challenged Judy and me to develop a purpose statement for our family, the exercise caused us to reexamine our priorities, our beliefs, and our behavior. If we were going to post our "constitution" where everyone—including our children—could see it, we wanted it to be a standard that accurately reflected our deepest beliefs and commitments. After a lot of thinking and composing, this is the statement that wound up on our kitchen wall:

> *The mission of the Blue family*
> *is to further the kingdom of God*
> *by providing a solid spiritual foundation*
> *for our children;*

and by recognizing that we are not an end in ourselves,
but rather a sending agency, a support group,
an example to others, and a family
to more than just ourselves.

This statement served our family well as we raised our five children. But now our kids are grown. Our youngest is in college, and in the past few years, we've welcomed three sons-in-law and two grandchildren into our family. We've also seen significant growth in RBC, the business we started nearly twenty years ago. As we reflected on these changes, Judy and I realized that this new season in our lives called for a new purpose statement. Today, the "constitution" that hangs in our home is this:

The mission of Ron and Judy Blue is to use our God-given resources of time, talent, treasure, and truth to further the kingdom of God by:
- *growing individually in our faith*
- *growing together in our relationship*
- *maximizing our relationships with our immediate family*
- *providing leadership, vision, and challenge to RBC*
- *serving the body of Christ in our other spheres of influence*

The essence of our vision—to further the kingdom of God—has not changed. But our circumstances have. In order for our purpose statement to maintain its relevance for our daily lives, we had to rethink it. Chances are, we will find ourselves in still another position in five or ten years, and we may want to revise our mission statement again. A purpose statement is a standard, but in order for it to work effectively it needs to be flexible.

To develop your own personal mission statement for your marriage or your family, start with a long-term perspective. As Covey puts it, "Begin with the end in mind." Think about what you want your marriage to look like in ten, twenty, or even fifty years. Visualize your family relationships, your worldly achievements, your impact for God's kingdom and eternity. By focusing on the future, you can better understand the long-term result of your current decisions in terms of how you use your money, your time, and your talents or abilities.

Again, a purpose statement doesn't come together overnight. For Judy and me, the process involved six basic steps. You're welcome to borrow our formula or come up with one that works better for you:

1. *Talk.* Have a long conversation with your spouse in which you picture the future. What does that image tell you about your goals and priorities? What do you want to accomplish? What do you want to see happen? Take some time to jot down your impressions, recording those thoughts that seem important to both of you.

2. *Look at your list.* Do you see any common themes? What are the main goals and ideas represented? Edit and revise your thoughts. Rewrite the main points into a statement that is no more than three sentences.

3. *Let your statement sit.* Leave it alone for a few days so you have time to really think about what you have written.

4. *Look at it again.* Try to edit your thoughts even further, crafting a statement that is easy to remember. This is perhaps the hardest part, but the more complex your statement is, the more difficult it will be to follow and apply.

> *Put your "constitution" in a place where you will see it often and use it to reinforce your sense of purpose and help you make wise decisions.*

5. *Test it.* Read your statement to two or three people to see whether it makes sense to them and whether or not it fits your lifestyle. When Judy and I drafted our first mission statement, we showed it to our children. Since they would have to live with our new standard, we wanted the document to be acceptable and relevant to them as well as to us.

6. *Make it visible.* Judy wrote our statement in calligraphy and had it framed to hang on our kitchen wall. You might want to write yours down on a piece of paper and tape it to your bathroom mirror. The point is to put your "constitution" in a place where you will see it often and use it to reinforce your sense of purpose and help you make wise decisions.

I have a friend named Todd who works in the financial consulting business. His wife Liz is a medical doctor and together they earn a healthy income. But when someone from their church approached them about participating in a multilevel marketing venture to earn extra money, they were intrigued. The church member told them how she had paid for her children to attend private school via her involvement in the venture. Todd and Liz could, she said, earn anywhere from $2,000 to $20,000 a year in additional income!

Todd listened politely to the woman's sales pitch, but when she was gone he turned to his wife. "Do we need more money?" he asked.

"No," Liz replied.

"Do we need more time with each other?"

"Yes."

"Should we do this multilevel marketing thing?"

"No!" Todd and Liz laughed over how easy their decision was. They did not fault their church friend for her choice; she and her husband enjoyed plenty of time together, and earning extra money to send their children to private school was a high priority for them. But for Todd and Liz, making time for one another in the midst of their busy schedules was a more important goal—and one that was a cornerstone of their purpose statement.

Think back to the story we told you at the beginning of this chapter. I was excited about the career possibilities associated with our move to Dallas. Judy was willing to support my choice. Looking back, though, we realize the price we paid in terms of our relationship. I was an absent husband and father for much of the time. Years later, when we faced another career move that would have involved a great deal of traveling for me, we rejected the job. With a purpose statement to guide us, we had a better handle on our priorities. We declined the job offer with confidence, certain that we were doing the best thing for our marriage and family.

Unity in decision making is a priceless commodity. A marriage purpose statement is one of the best tools I know of to promote unity and facilitate healthy communication. If you have a purpose statement that you have created together, you can approach any issue from the same side of the fence. Instead of doing things "my way" or "your way," you do things "our way." You make choices based on which option best supports your long-term, big-picture purpose. Instead of being driven by emotions or circumstances, you have a sense of mission and direction about what you are trying to accomplish with your life.

Earlier in this chapter I said that there is no such thing as a money problem. As you work your way through this book—dealing with everything from a spouse who spends too much to in-laws who refuse to let go of the purse strings on your life—use your marriage purpose statement as the window through which you view each situation. Use it as a launching pad for communication, a hedge to keep discussion on course. And use it as a means to turn "money problems" into opportunities to sharpen your perspective, resolve conflict, and communicate with sincerity and success.

Chapter Two

Can We Talk?

A Short Course in Effective Communication

Laura Swenson looked around the room at her guests. When she and Scott had decided to throw a dinner party featuring a homespun version of television's "Newlywed" game show, they had no idea how much fun the evening would be. So far, they had learned everything from which zoo animal the husbands thought they most resembled to which Olympic sport the wives secretly wished they could medal in. Laura smiled to herself. This would certainly be a night to remember.

As Laura poured coffee, Scott introduced the next question. "Guys," he said, "Guess how your wives answered this one: My husband and I can talk about anything except _____."

Groans of mock protest arose from around the room. "Oh, that one's easy," said Joe, a friend of Scott and Laura's since their college days. "Rita and I can talk about anything except money."

"Yeah," echoed Matt, who lived next door to the Swensons. "Money. Specifically, how much money our wives spend, right, guys?"

Rita raised her eyebrows and looked pointedly at the men in the room. "Maybe it's not our overspending that's the problem. Maybe it's your under depositing!"

"Hey—" one of the husbands started to object.

"Okay, time-out!" Laura cheerfully interjected. "Who's ready for some cheesecake?"

My spouse and I can talk about anything except money." After almost thirty years of professional financial counseling, I've probably heard that line a half a million times. Money is a touchy subject for many couples. Financial discussions can bring out the worst in us: we attack, retreat, manipulate, capitulate, storm, sulk, and spend our way through relationships riddled with conflict and frustration.

But it doesn't have to be that way. By understanding the reasons for conflict and applying the right problem-solving principles, you can greatly reduce the potential for ongoing friction in your marriage. Successful conflict resolution demands two things: a mutual recognition of what caused the tension in the first place, and an effective strategy for diffusing animosity and restoring harmony to the relationship.

> *As husbands and wives, we come from different backgrounds. Sometimes we share a common view of how to handle money, but more often our perspectives set us apart from one another.*

In this chapter, Judy and I want to highlight some of the most common conflict causers, from differences in our backgrounds to differences in the way men and women are created. We'll also look at the ways men and women often respond to conflict, using both historical and contemporary illustrations. Finally, we want to share with you some guidelines you can use for effective communication and conflict resolution, both in your marriage and in your other personal and professional relationships.

THE WAY WE WERE

One of the most basic reasons for conflict is that, as husbands and wives, we come from different backgrounds. Sometimes we share a common view of how to handle money, but more often our perspectives set us apart from one another. We spend years shaping and honing our individual beliefs, watching the financial habits of our parents, friends, and mentors. Even when a couple agrees on a broad financial principle—such as the avoidance of debt or the importance of saving money—there are apt to be wide variations on how to interpret and apply these principles in everyday life.

Steve and Lisa were well aware of their different backgrounds; in fact, their distinct experiences were one of the things that initially attracted them to one another. Steve came from a family that had little regard for the things they saw as unnecessary or extravagant— things like new cars, designer clothes, and even extra pillows on the sofa. The question was not whether or not they could afford these things: Steve's father was a partner in a small accounting firm, where he earned a good salary and chose his investments carefully. Steve's family had plenty of money. They just did not want to spend it on anything they did not really need.

Lisa, on the other hand, grew up in a household where all of her needs (and most of her desires) met with almost instant gratification. The daughter of a successful physician, she enjoyed wearing fashionable clothes, vacationing at upscale resorts, and perfecting her tennis game on the country club courts. These things were not "luxuries" in her eyes; they were simply the stuff of everyday life.

When Lisa met Steve she was intrigued by his no-nonsense approach. Noting the easy way he wore his unremarkable clothes, she decided that he must be very sure of himself—a quality she greatly admired. For Steve's part, he found himself attracted by Lisa's sense of style: she opened a door to a world he had never considered. Their romance blossomed, and a year and a half later, they got married.

Fast-forward seven years. It's a blistering summer day and Lisa and her two young children are trying, unsuccessfully, to coax a breeze through the fan in the window. Hot and irritable, Lisa finally decides to turn on the air conditioning—for the first time that summer. Later that evening, Steve arrives home from work and finds Lisa cooking dinner. "Why is the air on?" he wants to know. "We're not even halfway through July!"

Seeing Lisa's withering look, Steve decides to drop the subject. The next morning, though, he notices a new coffeemaker on the kitchen counter. "What's this?" he asks.

"The old one finally broke," Lisa explains. "I picked up this one at the mall yesterday."

"How much did it cost?"

"Twenty-nine dollars. Is that a problem?"

"No," Steve says, helping himself to a cup of coffee. "Not really."

Lisa forgets their conversation until two weeks later, when she suddenly finds another coffeemaker on the counter. "Steve?" she calls. "Why do we have two coffeemakers?"

"I was driving by a yard sale when I saw that other one," Steve explains. "I got it for a dollar!"

No response.

"Hey." Steve grins. "I just wanted to show you the kind of value you can find, if you're willing to shop around."

Lisa laughs, almost in spite of herself. Inwardly, though, she wonders how much longer she can live like this, facing an inquisition over every dollar she spends. Seven years ago, when she pledged to "honor and obey" her husband, she never dreamed her vow would mean they wouldn't have curtains in their dining room, or that Steve wouldn't want to turn the heat on until December!

> *To help prevent or resolve the conflicts caused by different backgrounds, you have to be willing to relinquish your "rights" and expectations, focusing instead on your spouse and his or her needs.*

In the first chapter, I told you how much our relationship changed when Judy and I became committed to one another, rather than to the institution of marriage. To help prevent or resolve the conflicts caused by different backgrounds, you have to be willing to relinquish your "rights" and expectations, focusing instead on your spouse and his or her needs. As Philippians 2:3–4 puts it, "Do nothing out of selfish ambition or vain conceit, but in humility consider others better than yourselves. Each of you should look not only to your own interests, but also to the interests of others."

THE WAY WE ARE

In addition to the potential for conflict that stems from our different backgrounds, husbands and wives often face tension because of the distinct ways men and women tend to respond to various situations or stimuli. Judy and I have become fascinated by several Bible studies and other courses which underscore our God-given differences. One of our recent favorites are the *Five Aspects of a Man* and *Five Aspects of a Woman* studies by Barbara K. Mouser. As we have worked our way through this material, we have come to a new understanding of why we each think and behave the way we do.

The title of one of the most popular books on this subject says it all: *Men Are from Mars, Women Are from Venus*. Many of the conclusions that author John Gray draws echo what biblical scholars have been saying for generations: Men and women are inherently different. As the *Five Aspects* study puts it, "If you add up all the plusses and minuses, and the weaknesses and the strengths of both sexes, they will come out equal. The point is, the strengths and the weaknesses of man and woman are different." The study goes on to define these differences: "The man was created to be the leader. As a leader he tends to be more independent and objective—good characteristics for a protector and final decision-maker. The woman tends to be more cooperative, leadable, sensitive, and subjective ... Her sensitivity enables her to pick up lots of data the man misses, which she uses most effectively in petitioning and counseling the man."[1]

While we realize that the character traits assigned to men and women in the *Five Aspects* study are based on generalizations rather than absolutes, Judy and I have seen, firsthand, how these traits manifest themselves in our marriage. For instance, I spent many years resisting Judy's advice, chiefly because I could not fathom how she came to her conclusions. As a man, I needed to process facts in a logical sequence, systematically working my way through a problem before I could arrive at the solution. Judy, on the other hand, was able to skip from A to Z, intuitively sensing the answer. Eventually, once I factored in all the variables, I would realize she was right!

I still don't know how she sees the things I miss. As one pastor I heard put it, the Bible says that God put Adam into a deep sleep before he created Eve—but nowhere does it mention that God ever woke Adam up again! I know the pastor told this story as a joke, but for me personally, it makes a great point.

And in all seriousness, you don't have to read more than a few chapters of Genesis to find out when tension began cropping up in the marriage relationship. The trouble started with history's first couple. When Eve disobeyed God by eating the forbidden fruit, part of her curse was that "Your desire will be for your husband, and he will rule over you" (Genesis 3:16). As many scholars have pointed out, this desire makes marital tension inevitable: "Instead of expressing the woman's sexual desire for her husband (an unlikely result of the fall!), the *desire* spoken of here is a desire to usurp his leadership. That is, in addition to pain in childbearing, the curse on woman produces conflict between herself and her husband."[2]

Conflict, then, is not an "optional experience" in marriage. Having said that, the question centers on how we handle the tension and clear the road for healthy communication. As men and women, we use all sorts of tactics to confront or deal with conflict. Most of these, unfortunately, only make the problems worse in the long run.

HOW MEN HANDLE CONFLICT

When a man faces a confrontation with his wife, he typically responds in one of three ways. Husbands, which one of these statements best describes the way you react?

1. I give in. I'd rather give up than fight.
2. I flee the scene, hoping the problem will take care of itself.
3. I assert my authority to gain control of the situation and get my way.

Unfortunately, when you give in, flee, or fight over your differences, you will never experience the satisfaction that comes with effective conflict resolution. Instead, you could find yourself sleeping on the floor. Consider what happened to a fellow I'll call Henry.

Henry was off on one of the frequent deep-sea fishing trips he liked to take with his buddies when Sarah went shopping for a new bed. Henry knew she had planned to make the purchase; they had even talked about an amount that they wanted to spend. The trouble started when Sarah found just the bed she was looking for—at more than twice the amount they had discussed.

Sarah did some quick math and figured out about how much Henry was spending for his fishing trip. The fact that he and his friends chartered a boat and took these trips several times a year served to strengthen her resolve. She bought the bed and had it set up in their bedroom when Henry returned.

"Gosh," Henry said. "That thing's huge. How much was it?"

"It's an antique."

"Yeah. So, how much was it?"

"Less than your old fishing boat."

"And that would be . . . ?"

When Sarah revealed the amount, Henry was speechless. He refused to discuss the subject, but that night, when Sarah climbed into bed, Henry did not join her. Instead, he made a pallet for himself and slept on the floor. Right under the big, new, expensive bed.

Henry's silent protest reminds me, in one sense, of how Pontius Pilate behaved when Jesus stood trial before him. As the story is recounted in Matthew 27, Pilate's wife sent him a message saying, "Don't have anything to do with that innocent man, for I have suffered a great deal today in a dream because of him." Ignoring his wife's counsel, Pilate gave in to the Jews' demand to crucify Jesus. He washed his hands in front of the crowd, signaling his desire to take no responsibility for the decision.

Professional counselor and author Larry Crabb traces this type of behavior to what he calls *The Silence of Adam*. In his book by that title, Crabb makes a convincing case that Adam was present in the Garden of Eden when Eve ate the forbidden fruit. Adam listened to every word the serpent spoke, watched Eve give in to temptation, *and said nothing*. "The silence of Adam is the beginning of every man's failure," Crabb writes, "from the rebellion of Cain to the impatience of Moses, from the weakness of Peter down to my failure yesterday to love my wife well."

Henry may have refused to sleep in the bed and Pilate may have symbolically washed his hands, but in both cases they did nothing—choosing, in essence, to *give up* rather than to *stand up* for their convictions. Crabb understands this behavior, pointing out that a man is "most comfortable in situations in which he knows exactly what to do. When things get confusing and scary, his insides tighten and he backs away. When life frustrates him with its maddening unpredictability, he feels the anger rise within him. And then, filled with terror and rage, he forgets God's truth and looks out for himself. From then on, everything goes wrong."[3]

Closely related to the "giving in" reaction is another of man's impulses: to flee from conflict. The writer of Proverbs certainly understood this temptation, noting that it is "better to live in a desert than with a quarrelsome and ill-tempered wife" (Proverbs 21:19). Men who run away from marital conflict take refuge in any number of places: they may work longer hours, play sports, or seek consolation and acceptance via an adulterous affair.

In the economic arena, the flight impulse manifests itself in men like George, who refused to take responsibility for his finances. Deep in debt, George and his wife Mary Ann were being hounded by their creditors as well as several IRS agents, who were after them to pay taxes they owed from several years back. They had already been forced to sell their home and move in with Mary Ann's parents. George was wondering whether they should declare bankruptcy. He wanted to talk it over with Mary Ann, but any financial discussion, he knew, was apt to turn into an argument. A fight was the last thing he wanted. Slipping the car keys into his pocket, he closed the screen door behind him and headed for the local tavern, where he looked forward to relaxing in the comfortable companionship of his friends.

Henry gave in. George left. Other men take a third approach to conflict resolution: they bully their wives into submission. Sometimes the desire to dominate manifests itself in verbal or physical abuse; in other cases, the control tactics are more subtle. Kevin, for example, took the steps he thought would ensure a marriage that was financially conflict-free. He kept the checkbooks, made all the deposits, paid the bills, and gave his wife Ginny a limited allowance for routine expenses like groceries and gasoline. She could not buy clothes for their children—or anything else, for that matter—without first clearing the purchase with him. Priding himself on his fiscal responsibility and "take-charge" leadership style, Kevin failed to recognize or acknowledge Ginny's growing bitterness toward the arrangement.

Giving in, running away, or fighting for control. Obviously, none of these three strategies is a desirable or effective way for a man to resolve conflict and promote harmony in his marriage. Neither are these responses unique to men. In fact, remember the curse in Genesis 3:16? It has come true. Ever since the Garden of Eden, women have been trying to dominate, control, outwit, or manipulate their husbands.

HOW WOMEN HANDLE CONFLICT

One of my coworkers recently returned from a family vacation where all of her in-laws and cousins had rented a large mountain cabin. My colleague, Jane, admired a new sweater her sister-in-law had purchased in the nearby village. "This is lovely!" she said. "Are you planning to wear it to dinner tonight?"

"Heavens no!" came the reply. "Stuart would *die* if he knew I bought a new sweater. I'm going to hang it in my closet for a few weeks before I break it out. That way, if he notices it, I can tell him the truth: It's not *new*; I just pulled it out of the closet!"

I asked Jane what she thought of her sister-in-law's behavior. "I doubt she was consciously trying to trick or dishonor her husband," Jane said. "I guess she just thinks Stuart is an old stick-in-the-mud when it comes to spending money—and she probably figures that what he doesn't know won't hurt him."

Jane's sister-in-law makes me think of Isaac's wife, Rebekah, whose story is told in Genesis 27. When it came time for Isaac to bless his son Esau, the firstborn of his twin sons, Rebekah had another plan in mind. She believed their other son, Jacob, should receive the blessing; he was her favorite—and besides, Esau's decision to marry foreign women had been a constant source of grief for their family.

Perhaps Rebekah truly thought she was doing the right thing. Perhaps, on the other hand, she recognized her deceitful motives and went ahead with her plan anyway. In any case, she hatched a scheme to secure the blessing for Jacob: First, Rebekah prepared a tasty meal for her husband (as Isaac had asked Esau to do). Next, she covered Jacob's smooth skin with goatskins and made him put on his brother's clothes so he would feel and smell like Esau. Finally, she sent him in to see Isaac. Being too old and blind to spot the deception, Isaac gave Jacob the blessing—only to discover his mistake moments later, when Esau belatedly arrived with the food *he* had prepared.

Rebekah thought her plan was better than Isaac's, and she used trickery and manipulation to get her way. In doing so, however, she alienated her husband and drove a wedge between her sons. Esau was so angry, in fact, that he vowed to kill his brother, and Rebekah was forced to send Jacob away for his own safety.

Other women forego such behind-the-scenes maneuvering in favor of a direct challenge. Sarah, for instance, decided she couldn't wait forever for God to fulfill his promise to her husband. The Lord had told Abraham that he would have as many children as the sky had stars, but so far, Sarah was barren—and she wasn't getting any younger. "The LORD has kept me from having children," she tells Abraham in Genesis 16:2. "Go, sleep with my maidservant; perhaps I can build a family through her."

Sarah's request was not unprecedented; many childless wives had "borne" children through their servants. But things didn't go as Sarah had planned. When Hagar, the maidservant, realized she was pregnant, she began to mock and despise Sarah. In distress, Sarah turned on her husband, challenging his wisdom and authority a second time. "You are responsible for the wrong I am suffering," she taunted. "May the LORD judge between you and me."

Once again, Abraham caved under the pressure. He told Sarah to do whatever she wanted to with Hagar. Sarah took that as a license to mistreat Hagar, who wound up taking refuge in the desert. You can read the rest of the story, including how God intervened to rescue Hagar, in Genesis 16.

A third way women behave toward men is not by trying to manipulate or challenge them, but by trying to please them—even if it means saying or doing something they shouldn't. Acts 5 recounts the story of Ananias and Sapphira, two early churchgoers who tried to pull a fast one on the apostles. At the time, all the believers were one in heart and mind, sharing their possessions and everything they had. As Acts 4:34–35 tells it, people even sold their land or houses and gave the money to the apostles to meet the needs of their fellow Christians.

Everything was running smoothly until Ananias decided to sell some property. "With his wife's full knowledge," Acts 5:2 says, "he kept back part of the money for himself, but brought the rest and put it at the apostles' feet." Ananias was probably expecting a big pat on the back for his contribution, but Peter knew the real story. "Ananias," Peter said, "how is it that Satan has so filled your heart that you have lied to the Holy Spirit and have kept for yourself some of the money you received for the land? . . . What made you think of doing such a thing? You have not lied to men but to God."

What happened next is nothing short of remarkable. Ananias fell down and died, right there at Peter's feet. Amazed (and more than a little frightened by the experience), some young fellows came in, got Ananias's body, and buried him.

Three hours later Sapphira showed up. Not knowing what had happened to her husband, perhaps she wondered at Peter's question: "Tell me," he said, "is this the price you and Ananias got for the land?" No sooner had Sapphira confirmed the false price than she too fell down and died.

> *Women aren't the only ones who manipulate and challenge their spouses, just as men aren't the only ones who fight or flee.*

The Bible doesn't tell us whether Sapphira was a schemer like her husband, or whether she was just trying to cover up for his lie. Either way, she went along with Ananias's plan, knowing all along that it was wrong. She stood by her man—and paid with her life.

Whatever their good points may have been, Rebekah was a manipulator, Sarah an open challenger, and Sapphira a man-pleaser. Wives, can you identify with any of these women? When you disagree with your husband about something, which one of these responses best describes your approach to the situation?

1. I try to get the upper hand through manipulation or hiding the facts.
2. I challenge my husband—especially when I think I know better.
3. I pretty much do as he says; things seem to go more smoothly that way.

Again, women aren't the only ones who manipulate and challenge their spouses, just as men aren't the only ones who fight or flee. But it should come as no surprise that none of these options will promote long-term satisfaction or peace in a relationship. Let's look, then, at God's design for effective communication and conflict resolution in marriage.

STRATEGIES FOR EFFECTIVE CONFLICT RESOLUTION

In the last chapter we focused on God's intentions for the marriage relationship. When husbands and wives commit to one another (rather than to the relationship itself), we see the outworkings of Christ's relationship with the church, as described in Ephesians 5:28–29: "He who loves his wife loves himself. After all, no one ever hated his own body, but he feeds and cares for it, just as Christ does the church."

Scripture commands husbands to selflessly love their wives, and wives to respect their husbands. It's not difficult to see how, in a perfect world in which these commandments were never broken, marriages would be peaceful, satisfying, uplifting relationships. But we don't live in a perfect world. We live in a fallen world, and our natural tendencies are to focus on ourselves and attempt to impose our will on others.

We've already seen what can happen when conflict is resolved in an inadequate or ineffective manner. From Rebekah's deceitful quest to manipulate Isaac to my selfish attempt, not long ago, to get Judy to do something "my" way, communication breakdowns often leave ugly scars. Wounded relationships, broken families, and a discouraging lack of peace and satisfaction are just a few of the consequences that can mar a marriage.

In order to maintain our commitment to loving, cherishing, and honoring our spouse, we need to yield ourselves and our rights, first to God and then to one another. Over the years, Judy and I have used several strategies to help prevent communication stalemates, blowouts, and breakdowns. If you and your spouse have a difference of opinion, try approaching conflict with one or more of these guidelines in mind:

Stick to the Problem at Hand

Instead of bringing up past wrongs with comments such as "You always . . ." and "You never . . . ," focus on the current conflict. Putting your spouse on the defensive is never a good idea when you're trying to reach an agreement.

Get on the Same Side of the Fence

Instead of approaching an issue "my way" or "your way," work toward a solution that represents "our way." (Your marriage purpose statement can help with this objective.)

Try to Identify the Core Issue

Conflict often results from a series of events or issues that can disguise the real problem. Look at the attitudes or beliefs that motivate your behavior and opinions for clues as to what the core issue in any conflict is.

Don't Be a Mind Reader

Don't expect your spouse to know or guess what you are thinking.

Don't try to analyze your spouse's thoughts or motives; instead, ask direct questions about his or her behavior. Likewise, don't expect your spouse to know or guess what you are thinking. Talk openly about your beliefs and expectations.

Don't Let the Sun Go Down on Your Anger

Settling disputes is never fun; it takes hard work and a mutual commitment to problem solving. It can also take time. If you haven't reached an agreement by bedtime, put the matter aside with the understanding that you will resume discussion the next day. As Ephesians 4:27 warns, holding on to anger overnight gives the devil a foothold in your life. Don't leave yourself (or your marriage) vulnerable.

Avoid Character Assassination

When you work on conflict resolution, it's okay to talk about circumstances and behavior. It's not okay, however, to attack your spouse's personality or character.

Remember That Love Keeps No Record of Wrongs

Be quick to forgive, quick to admit your own mistakes, and quick to move on from the conflict.

One final note belongs here. Bookstore shelves are full of "how-to" books from popular psychologists and other communication gurus. While they may have some good advice to offer, nothing beats the Bible when it comes to arming yourself with wisdom for daily living. Consider these communication jewels: "Everyone should be quick to listen, slow to speak and slow to become angry" (James 1:19). "Do not let any unwholesome talk come out of your mouths, but only what is helpful for building others up according to their needs, that it may benefit those who listen" (Ephesians 4:29). "Clothe yourselves with compassion, kindness, humility, gentleness and patience. Bear with each other and forgive whatever grievances you may have against one another. Forgive as the Lord forgave you" (Colossians 3:12–13).

Tonight, before you go to bed, get out a Bible and look up one of these verses, or find another one that speaks to you. Copy the verse or commit it to memory, asking God to make it real in your life. Then, when conflict arises in your marriage because of your different backgrounds, your different perspectives, or something else, use your verse to help you respond wisely to the situation.

In the next chapter, we'll look at another strategy for furthering communication: the planning weekend. Equipped with the communication principles outlined in this chapter, you can plan a marriage getaway that will refresh your relationship and enable you to focus on the financial goals and other objectives that matter most in your marriage.

─ Chapter Three ────────────────────────────

Stoking the Fire

Planning Weekends and Other Strategies
for Ongoing Dialogue

J im, have you seen the electric bill?"

From where he stood, shaving his face before the bathroom mirror, Jim Patterson could hear his wife rummaging through their kitchen, opening drawers and shuffling through the stack of magazines, letters, and other mail that always piled up next to the telephone.

"I thought you mailed it yesterday," Jim called, rinsing his razor.

"No, I couldn't find it. I mailed all the other bills." Carol poked her head through the bathroom door. "That painter who did the Wilson's house last summer is coming by to give us an estimate this afternoon. And don't forget your dentist appointment at 4:15—they called yesterday to confirm it."

The dentist! Jim had forgotten—although he wasn't about to admit it to Carol. The painter was another matter. "I thought we agreed that we couldn't afford to paint the house right now," he said.

"Well, I thought we should at least get some estimates." Carol turned back toward the kitchen. "Can you pick the boys up from soccer practice tonight? I promised to help with the decorations for the church bazaar, and I might be a little late getting home. There's a chicken casserole in the refrigerator—and oh, that reminds me, I think we need to up our grocery allowance. Last week I had to dip into the gas money to pay for everything. And I didn't have enough cash left to pay the piano teacher."

Jim followed Carol into the kitchen and picked up his briefcase. "Okay— except that I'm not sure where the money's going to come from. Maybe we can figure something out next week when I get back from Cleveland."

"You're going to Cleveland?"

"For the managers' meeting, remember? I know I told you about it."

"Yeah, you probably did. Anyhow, I've got to run or the kids will be late for school. Boys! Come on down; we've got to go!" Carol headed toward the door and then stopped. "Have you seen my car keys? I could have sworn I put them right there on the counter!"

These days, you don't have to have a problem communicating to have a communication problem. Juggling careers, children, church and school functions, sporting events, volunteer activities, and an endless list of other commitments and "to-do" items leaves many couples feeling like they hardly ever *see* one another, let alone find the time to actually *talk*.

You don't have to have a problem communicating to have a communication problem.

At the outset of this book I told you how having a marriage purpose statement could give your relationship meaning and direction. In chapter two, we looked at the different ways men and women handle conflict and discussed some strategies for fostering healthy communication. But without a game plan for putting your purpose statement into action and keeping communication on track, these tools could easily wind up rusting in the toolbox, casualties of the more *urgent* (but not necessarily more *important*) things in life.

Twenty years ago, Judy and I heard Howie Hendricks, Dallas Theological Seminary's well-known author and speaker, talk about the importance of setting goals for your marriage. I had only been a Christian for a few years, and up to that point, Judy and I had taken a "buckshot" approach to our marriage, spraying our combined firepower at everything from raising our children to managing a career in full-time ministry. Pursuing these loosely defined objectives, we occasionally hit our targets—but we also pegged a lot of other stuff that we never really aimed for in the first place.

Judy and I realized we needed to take a more focused approach to our marriage and our goals if we were ever to make any significant progress in either area. We wanted to do more than just *survive* in our marriage; we wanted to *thrive*. We wanted to build a relationship that would glorify God and allow us to actively pursue the aims he had for us, instead of just chasing after the things that we thought would add pleasure or satisfaction to our lives.

After hearing Hendricks speak several more times, we finally approached him to ask whether he had any tools we could use to help us evaluate our lives and plot a course for the future. He gave us a questionnaire to complete and an assignment: We were to clear our calendars for a getaway weekend that included a strong dose of work and planning, along with a healthy chunk of time for leisure and romance.

It was a weekend that changed our lives.

A WEEKEND THAT COULD CHANGE YOUR LIVES

A planning weekend is, in essence, a weekend away from the children where couples can establish goals and plan for the future while enjoying spiritual refreshment, romantic pursuits, and a change of environment. It doesn't matter whether your budget allows for a room in a motel just across town or a cozy cabin in a mountain resort area. Any retreat will do, although it helps to pick a place that offers appropriate recreational facilities. The weekend should be a good mix of work and play.

Before you go, plan your schedule for the weekend. While your first getaway will be your most important session, think long term and schedule follow-up weekends for the future. Hendricks recommends that couples retreat every four months to maintain good communication and keep their marriages fresh and vital. If you can't commit to this trimester plan, put a planning weekend on your calendar at least once a year, if not every six months.

Here is a suggested schedule for your weekend, which we have adapted from a similar weekend agenda originally detailed in my book *Storm Shelter*. This is not meant to be a hard-and-fast routine; rather, it is simply a format that has worked well for Judy and me. Feel free to make revisions to suit your individual needs, but remember to allow plenty of time for communication.

SUGGESTED SCHEDULE FOR
A GOAL-SETTING WEEKEND

Friday Evening

Begin your planning weekend with a relaxed, unstructured evening. Don't try to make any plans or set any goals; rather, simply enjoy spending time together. Take time to pray together; prayer is what will make the difference between a weekend of wishful thinking (or selfish dreaming) and one that allows you to focus on purposeful, deliberate, God-given goals and strategies for your lives.

Saturday Morning

Take time apart from one another to go through the Planning Questionnaire on pages 41–44. As you answer the questions, think about which ones matter most to you and how they might eventually translate into specific goals. Feel free to revise the questions or add different ones that might apply to your individual relationship and circumstances.

Lunch Break

Take a break from the questionnaire and relax. Go for a walk or enjoy some other kind of recreation before you start your afternoon session.

Saturday Afternoon

Complete the questionnaire and get together with your spouse to compare notes. Are there questions or issues that matter to both of you? Are there obvious differences in the things that each of you sees as important? Talk through your answers and conclude your time with prayer.

Saturday Evening

Put your questionnaires on the back burner and let the information "simmer" while you and your spouse enjoy dinner, recreation, and romance.

Sunday Morning

After breakfast, spend some time praying together and reading a passage of Scripture. This can be a formal devotional time, planned in advance of your weekend, or an impromptu worship experience.

Get out your questionnaires, along with the Goal-Setting Worksheet. Your job is to use the answers recorded on your questionnaires as a springboard for prayerfully developing goals in the six major categories: spiritual, financial, marriage, family, social, and physical. Again, adapt this worksheet to meet your own needs; not every couple will want to pursue goals in each of these six areas, and there may be other categories (such as vocational or intellectual goals) that you want to concentrate on.

Resolve to set (and pursue) at least one goal in each category. It will help if you write your goals in terms that can be measured or quantified: for example, in the financial category, your goal may be "to get out of debt within the next three years" or "to establish a college savings plan for our children and contribute at least X dollars each month for the next eight years."

Break for lunch on Sunday, and then continue your goal-setting if you have more information you want to cover.

As the suggested agenda indicates, a significant portion of your weekend will be spent working through the Planning Questionnaire and the Goals Worksheet. You can use the questionnaire and worksheet included in this chapter, or revise them to address your specific needs. Either way, the chief purpose of these tools is to help you identify areas you want to work on and communicate about various subjects—including those where you and your spouse don't always agree.

PLANNING QUESTIONNAIRE

The questions and categories listed on this questionnaire are not meant to be all-inclusive. Adapt, ignore, or supplement them as you need to. Don't try to pinpoint any "right" or "wrong" answers; rather, use this document as a catalog of ideas to jump-start your goal-setting process and help you understand and appreciate your spouse's thoughts and priorities. Record your answers on a separate sheet of paper.

Financial Questions

___Do I feel comfortable with the amount of money we make?

___Is there anything we can do to improve our financial situation?

___Do we have an adequate amount of life insurance? What about home, health, and auto coverage? Do I know how to locate and use the policy information?

___Do we need to reduce our taxes? Are we under- or over-withholding?

___Are we giving away the right amount or percentage of our income? Are our gifts being used for the right purposes or organizations? When is the best time for us to give—weekly, monthly, or on some other schedule?

___How much debt do we have? Is this an acceptable amount? Should we try to get out of debt, or avoid it altogether?

___How much are we saving? How much should we be saving? What are we saving for? How often should we set money aside, and where should we put it?

___Why are we investing? How much should we invest? Am I comfortable with how our investment portfolio is allocated? Should we be more (or less) aggressive in our investment approach?

___How much should we spend on things like our house, our vacations, our cars, etc.?

___Do we want to send our children to private/Christian school? How much will that cost? How much are we willing/able to spend on a college education for our children?

Marriage Questions

___Is our marriage headed in the right direction? Are we growing closer and is the relationship maturing?

___Am I meeting my spouse's emotional, physical, and intellectual needs?

___Is my spouse meeting my emotional, physical, and intellectual needs?

___Do we clearly communicate with one another?

___Should we go out more often, or make more time for romance?

___Do I tell my spouse "I love you" often enough? What do I do or say to show my love?

___What can we do to improve our sexual relationship?

___What do we want our marriage to look like five years from now?

___What do I see as the husband's primary responsibilities in the marriage relationship?

___What do I see as the wife's primary responsibilities in the marriage relationship?

Family Questions

___How many children would we like to have?

___Do we consistently and properly love our children?

___Do we consistently and properly discipline them?

___What are the most important character traits we want to see our children develop?

___What rules do we want to establish for our children at home and in public?

___Where should we go on vacation? How should we spend weekends and other leisure time?

___Does our devotion to our children interfere with or hamper our marriage relationship?

___If something were to happen to us, who would we want to serve as the guardian for our children? Have we provided for our children through a will?

___Do we support one another in front of our children?

___According to the following passages, what are the main responsibilities of parents and children? Colossians 3:20–21; Hebrews 12:5–11; Proverbs 3:11–12; Ephesians 6:4.

Spiritual Questions

___Am I spending consistent, quality time with the Lord? Is my spiritual relationship stagnant or progressive?

___Should we have family devotions? What should they look like?

___Am I providing spiritual encouragement for my spouse?

___Should we be more involved in personal evangelism?

___Are we active in our church?

___What are my primary spiritual gifts?

___What are my spouse's primary spiritual gifts?

___Are we effectively using these gifts for the kingdom of God?

___What can we do to improve our prayer life, individually and as a couple?

___What should our ministry focus be?

Social Questions

___Is there a proper balance between my time spent at home and away from home?

___Should we entertain more?

___Should we be making an effort to get to know more people?

___Are there any specific people I would like to get to know better?

___Are we involved in our community, schools, and/or social organizations?

___Are we overcommitted to social, athletic, or other activities?

___Do our children demonstrate wisdom when choosing their friends?

___Do we demonstrate wisdom when choosing friends and social activities?

___Are there people in the church and neighborhood that we should help, befriend, and care for?

___Is our home an inviting place for our friends and our children's friends to gather?

Physical Questions

___How can I improve my eating habits?

___How can we improve our family's eating habits?

___Are we getting enough exercise?

___Is my spouse getting enough exercise?

___Are our children involved in athletic or physical activities?

___Are there any skills or sports I want to learn (i.e., to play the piano, speak French, or play tennis)?

___Do I need to lose/gain weight?

___Is there anything I should do to make myself more attractive to my spouse?

___Are there any athletic goals I want to pursue (i.e., being able to run a mile—or a marathon)?

___What can I do to encourage or enable my spouse to meet his/her physical goals?

CATEGORY	GOAL (*What* you want to accomplish)	PROGRAMS/HELPS (*How* you can accomplish it)	SCHEDULE (*When* you want to achieve it)
Financial			
Marriage			
Family			
Spiritual			
Physical			

GOALS WORKSHEET

The worksheet on page 45 is designed to be used with the Planning Questionaire. Using your answers to the questions, identify at least one goal in each category that you want to pursue. Since the best goals are written in well-defined, measurable terms, this worksheet includes space for recording "how" and "when" you would like to accomplish your goals. (Again, feel free to add or delete categories to tailor this worksheet to your specific needs.)

During one of our first planning weekends, Judy and I discovered a problem with our bill-paying system. Judy is naturally more detail-oriented than I am, so it seemed to make sense for her to write the checks and mail the bills each month. What neither of us initially recognized, though, is that this arrangement created an unnecessary fear in Judy's mind. At the time, our personal finances were closely tied to the financial planning business I had just launched. As a financial planner, I had mapped out a strategy for the business as well as for our family, and I focused my thoughts on where we could expect to be in five or ten years. I looked at the big picture. Moreover, I was working on a commission basis, and I kept track of our current income as well as the payments I knew I would receive in the months to come.

Judy, on the other hand, focused on how much (or little) we had in our bank account. Unwilling to let the bills pile up, she paid each one almost as soon as it arrived in our mailbox. Since our checkbook register showed a lean balance from time to time, the steady need for check-writing became a small but constant threat to Judy's financial peace of mind. She was acutely aware of how much we spent each month, and every check she wrote chipped away at her sense of financial security.

As we worked together on our questionnaire, one of the questions brought Judy's fear and dissatisfaction to the surface. At first, I failed to appreciate her distress. I wondered why she had such a problem with what I considered an easy, routine job. But as we talked through the issue and I began to see things from Judy's perspective, it all started to make sense. In the end, we decided that I should take over the bill-paying responsibility.

I wish I could say that this decision marked the end of our bill-paying problems. In reality, though, the transition took some time. We both know that Judy is more disciplined than I am, and it was difficult for her, at first, to hand over the financial reins without always wanting to peek over my shoulder to be sure that I hadn't forgotten to pay the telephone bill. With time, though, *and as we continued to talk through our concerns*, we both gained confidence in our new system.

Putting these plans into practice, however, requires a commitment to ongoing communication.

I emphasize our continued discussion to illustrate the need to make the goals and revelations that come out of your planning weekends a part of your day-to-day living. Planning weekends are like presidential summit meetings; you can come up with some excellent policies, goals, and objectives. Putting these plans into practice, however, requires a commitment to ongoing communication. You need to stage some "mini-summits" to keep your plans on track.

THREE MINI-SUMMIT STRATEGIES THAT REALLY WORK

Judy and I have considered any number of ways and places to hold our mini-summit meetings. One of our longest-running and most effective communication techniques has become more of a habit than a strategy. Each morning when we get up, Judy and I don't leave our bedroom without spending about fifteen minutes talking to one another. Sometimes we focus on the day ahead, verbally walking each other through any special appointments or needs we have. Often we share our concerns for our children or insights from our personal quiet times. We've even used our morning time to tackle unresolved issues or disagreements in an attempt to "finish the fight."

In a tradition that has grown stronger over the years, we make a point to get up early, so that this time is uninterrupted and uncluttered by the pressures of the day. (It's getting easier now that our kids are grown.) Alone in our retreat, we find time to talk, pray, and encourage one another before the day begins. It's only a few minutes, but as a communication tool, it's terrific.

A second strategy favored by many couples and recommended by most marriage experts is regularly scheduled date nights. It doesn't matter what season of life you are in. Every married couple—from newlyweds to empty nesters—should put a date night on the calendar at least twice a month, if not weekly.

What do you do on a date night? Judy and I have enjoyed everything from dinner at a favorite restaurant to an afternoon "date night" on the golf course. You could go bowling, play checkers, take a leisurely stroll through your neighborhood, or browse through a bookshop and then find a spot for coffee or dessert. One couple we know likes to curl up by the fire and read aloud to one another. The point is this: You can do almost anything on a date night, as long as you follow these guidelines:

1. Pick an outing or activity that you both enjoy.

2. Make sure to leave room for conversation during your date. While date nights are designed for relaxation and romance, they also afford an excellent opportunity to revisit the goals and ideas you established during your planning weekend. (In other words, catching a movie and then dashing home to pay the baby-sitter doesn't count.)

3. Double dating is not allowed. It's fine—and fun—to go out with other couples, but not when you want to focus on each other or when you want to talk about things like your financial, physical, or spiritual goals. As one marriage counselor put it, "You can't expect intimacy in a group-oriented environment. Typically, the men talk to the men, the women talk to the women, and by the end of the evening, you have hardly spoken to your spouse!"

A third mini-summit strategy Judy and I use is a weekly business meeting. In the business world, weekly meetings are an indispensable way to coordinate schedules, compare progress reports, and let each member of a group know what the other members are doing.

With five children and seven different schedules to coordinate, Judy and I discovered the value of weekly business meetings years ago. Once a week we get out our calendars and compare notes on our activities and commitments. In addition to helping us manage the details of our lives, these meetings enable us to stay focused on our short- and long-term goals. Using our calendars as a working tool, we can spot (and try to delete) those things which threaten to pull us off course. We can also look down the road to discover each other's special needs—such as the need for prayer and encouragement when one of us is scheduled to speak before a group or participate in an important meeting.

With five children and seven different schedules to coordinate, Judy and I discovered the value of weekly business meetings years ago.

Sometimes, too, the calendar alerts us to the problem of over-commitment. On more than one occasion I've advised Judy (or she's advised me) not to take on a particular project or responsibility, no matter how worthwhile it appears. And calendars are often a vital asset in the budgeting process. If you know a special event or holiday is coming up, having it marked on the calendar can help you plan your finances to avoid the problems of overspending and indebtedness.

Morning talks, date nights, and weekly business meetings are just three ways you can encourage communication in your marriage. No doubt you will discover other strategies that can work just as well. But no matter how or when you choose to hold your mini-summits, your toughest obstacle will always be *time*. I speak from experience. When Howie Hendricks first suggested that Judy and I devote a few hours each week to communicating about our lives and goals, we wondered how we would find the time. Could we afford that many hours—or even minutes—away from the children, my job, and the various responsibilities of running our lives?

When we turned the question around, though, it took on a whole new significance. If we wanted our relationship to be growing, vibrant, and purposeful, the question we had to ask ourselves was not "How can we afford to spend this much time together?" but "How can we afford *not* to find the time for communication?"

Make the time. As Judy and I continue to discover, the results in terms of the quality of our relationship and the effectiveness of our lives more than justify the effort. Using the tools provided here—the

Planning Weekend Agenda, the Pre-Planning Questionnaire, and the Goals Worksheet—you can build a framework for communication that will allow you to strengthen your relationship even as you tackle the inevitable conflicts and problems that every marriage faces.

The remainder of this book is devoted to finding solutions for some of the most common financial problems in marriage. Hardly a day goes by when I don't talk to someone who is struggling with indebtedness, investment uncertainty, or unanswered questions about everything from estate planning to tithing. Yet in each of these situations, the problem is not about money. It's about having the right perspective and knowing how to communicate effectively. In the next seven chapters, I want to show you exactly what I mean when I say, again, that there is no such thing as a money problem.

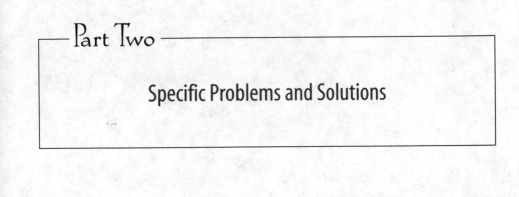

Part Two

Specific Problems and Solutions

Chapter Four

Divorce Your Money Problems, Not Your Spouse

Budget Basics for a Happy Home

There it was, in black and white, but Ray didn't trust what he saw. Rubbing his eyes, he looked at the papers again, this time holding them at arm's length. Yes, it was true. The quarterly statement he received from his brokerage firm indicated that his portfolio had jumped nearly twenty percent in value.

Ray knew the stock market had been good—anybody who had bothered to pick up a newspaper in the last several months could tell you that. But, until now, he had had no idea just how good, or what the climbing Dow would actually mean to him. In just three months, Ray's investments had earned $22,000. Engrossed in the figures, he hardly noticed when his wife, Martha, slipped into the room and set a small tea tray on his desk.

"And hello there to you, too," Martha said, feigning a pout as she picked up the teapot and began to pour.

"What? Oh—" Ray cleared his throat. "Thank you, darling. I'm sorry I didn't hear you. But I've got some pretty good news. Take a look at this."

Martha glanced at the brokerage report and her eyes widened in surprise. "That's quite a healthy jump, isn't it?"

"Quite," Ray agreed, accepting the steaming mug Martha offered.

"I guess this means we can go ahead and call the architect, eh? I've been running some terrific ideas around in my head—I can hardly wait to see it all on paper." Martha's blue eyes danced as she spoke, revealing an enthusiasm that Ray found hard to resist. "If we start soon," she continued, "I bet we can have everything finished by Christmastime. Won't it be wonderful to have a place for the grandchildren to play?"

"Whoa, girl," Ray said, raising his hands. "Hold your horses. It's not like we've won the lottery or anything. All this represents is $22,000.

Before taxes. And we're going to need every bit of that just to get within shooting distance of retirement."

"Ray . . ." Martha sunk to her chair, unable to mask her disappointment. "Honey, we've been talking about that addition for years. You know we need the room, especially when the kids are home. And we're not getting any younger—if we don't do it now, then when?"

"Hrmph. You don't have to remind me how old we are."

Martha studied her husband's face, reading the concern in his eyes. At sixty-one, he was approaching retirement with more uncertainty than enthusiasm. He often said he wished they'd started saving earlier. Martha sighed. How much money did you have to have before you could retire? At this rate, she figured, they would probably never build that addition.

It doesn't matter how much money you make. It doesn't matter whether you want to buy a starter home or a retirement home, or whether your idea of a big treat is to buy tickets to the movies or tickets on a cruise line. No matter how much money you have, and no matter how much more you can earn, there will always be unlimited ways to allocate limited resources.

> *No matter how much money you have, and no matter how much more you can earn, there will always be unlimited ways to allocate limited resources.*

For married couples, few truths can be more unsettling. It's hard enough deciding how to spend money when you have only your own needs and wants to consider—how much more complicated it gets when you add another person's perspective to the mix! Where one spouse wants to save, the other often wants to spend. Where one spouse squirrels away nuts for the winter, the other eyes the bigger trees in the forest, hoping to find a better place to eat the nuts.

As Judy and I started to work on this chapter, I ran into a colleague who serves as the managing partner of a CPA firm in Baltimore. When he asked what I was up to, I told him: "My wife and I are writing a book about money and marriage. The chapter we're into now is on budgeting."

My colleague let out a laugh. "Marriage? Budgeting? Isn't that an oxymoron?"

Frankly, I'm not surprised by his reaction. Most people see marriage and money management as sort of an oil-and-water mix. But that doesn't negate the need for a strategic spending plan. Take a moment to answer a few questions and I think you'll see what I mean:

Have you and your spouse ever argued over financial matters?

Have you ever impulsively bought a car or major appliance?

Do you routinely fail to balance your checkbook?

Do you bounce checks more than once a year, or do you frequently rely on an overdraft protection credit line?

Have you ever tried using a budget, but given up after only a few weeks or months?

Do you occasionally or frequently receive past due notices?

Do you use credit cards for car repairs or other emergency expenses?

Are your credit cards at or near their limit?

Do you use credit cards to meet your living expenses (groceries, eating out, etc.)?

Do you routinely pay only the minimum amount due on credit accounts?

Have you ever considered or received a consolidation loan?

Do you frequently dip into savings to meet expenses?

Do you have less than three months' worth of living expenses in cash available in savings or money market funds?

Have you ever borrowed money from friends or relatives and failed to repay the loan according to the agreed terms?

Do you worry or lose sleep over the level of your mortgage?

Have you had any bills turned over to a collection agency?

If you answered "yes" to more than three of these questions, your future financial security may be at risk. A budget can help safeguard your finances—and strengthen your marriage in the process. I'm not saying you have to start hoarding your pennies, slicing expenses, and cutting out all the fun. Instead, I want to encourage you to develop a plan for effective spending—one that allows you to allocate your resources among the best possible alternatives to help you meet your short- and long-term goals. The sooner you start planning, the better.

WHY SPENDING PLANS WORK:
FIVE GOOD REASONS TO GET YOU STARTED

The number one reason for couples to develop a spending plan—a budget—is to reduce conflict in their marriage.

"What's that?" you say. "Budgeting can *reduce* marital conflict?" I can just see all you "My-spouse-and-I-can-talk-about-anything-but-money" people scratching your heads—but hear me out. Budgeting reduces conflict for the simple reason that it provides built-in accountability and an objective standard for all of your spending decisions.

You might be surprised by how many financial transactions you make. If you add up all the checks you write, all the credit card purchases you make, and everything you pay cash for, you could easily make 1,500 or 2,000 transactions a year. With or without a budget, you are going to spend money, whether it's to buy groceries, pay the rent, or take a family vacation. If you don't have a budget—a spending plan that allocates your income to reflect your priorities—any one of these expenditures could touch off an argument. In fact, if you only disagree about one out of every one hundred purchases, you will wind up at odds with your spouse at least once a month. Statistically speaking, money fights or frustrations are a virtual certainty!

Judy and I use a computer software program to track our purchases. According to the computer, we make anywhere from two to three thousand transactions each year. But since most of our spending decisions are premade in our family budget, there is very little disagreement about where our money should go. As a result, we have the freedom and flexibility to enjoy our purchases without fear, guilt, or conflict. Our budget works to eliminate potential problems before they arise.

The second reason why a spending plan makes sense is that it allows you to create and maintain a vision for the future. A budget gives you the guidelines you need to successfully spend less than you earn—which, as any financial analyst can tell you, is the key to long-term financial security. Whether you want to buy a home, start your own business, fund your children's college education, or set yourself up for a comfortable retirement, a spending plan can keep you focused on your goals.

Third, a spending plan means that nobody has to be the bad guy. As I mentioned earlier, most marriages usually have a spending spouse and a saving spouse. Any time the spender buys something, he or she becomes a potential target: *Why did you buy that? It costs too much! And we don't really need it. Couldn't you have found something less expensive?* Likewise, when the saver refuses to spend money, he or she may invite criticism: *Why can't we buy that? It's not that expensive—and besides, it's on sale. You worry about money too much. Don't be such a killjoy.*

> *A spending plan means that nobody has to be the bad guy.*

When a budget is in place, it becomes the standard. Objective and impartial, the spending plan draws a line between the affordable and the out-of-reach, the wise purchase and the foolish. Because a budget is drafted with input from both spouses, the spending/saving decisions are not "mine" or "yours," but "ours." We're on the same side of the fence.

A fourth reason why we recommend a spending plan is that it forces couples to communicate. You can't establish budget categories and allocate income without talking about priorities, needs, dreams, and goals. Fears and insecurities can also be part of the process—as when Judy confessed her dislike for the monthly bill-paying responsibility. By providing a forum for discussion, the budgeting process enables you to define and address philosophical differences—including everything from how much to spend on food and clothing to how, where, or when you want to give money to your children, your church, or your charity.

Finally, by establishing and using a budget you set a great example for your kids. As Judy and I often remind ourselves, "More is caught than taught." When your children see you exercising financial discipline and making progress toward your goals, they will learn a valuable lesson about how to handle their own money.

Reducing conflict, creating vision, eliminating the bad guy, fostering communication, and demonstrating wise money management are all good reasons to develop a spending plan. But I'm not pretending that the process will be easy. At times it might even be a struggle. It's like going for a swim in the ocean: you have to get through a few rough spots before you get past the breakers. But I can promise you one thing: Once you get beyond the turbulence and out to where the water is gentle and clear, you will never want to go back.

CREATING AND USING A BUDGET YOU CAN LIVE WITH

You live with your spouse. You need to be just as comfortable living with your spending plan. Just as the things we think of as "money problems" are really a reflection of other, non-economic issues, so a spending plan is not strictly a financial matter. How you allocate your resources is driven by your individual priorities, values, and goals. In the last chapter you considered your short- and long-term goals. You will want to keep this information handy as you develop and customize your individual family budget.

The information and worksheets included in this chapter are designed to get you started on the budgeting process. If you would like more information, my book *Master Your Money* offers an in-depth look at financial planning. You may also wish to purchase a computer software program to help you keep track of your finances. There are many very good programs on the market.

In the remaining pages of this chapter we will outline a simple, four-step process you can use to draft and implement your budget. As you read and discuss this information with your spouse, choose a time that you both find convenient to complete the worksheets and share your insights with one another. Don't be like the young couple we heard about recently. A few weeks before their wedding, as they reviewed their honeymoon plans, the groom turned to his bride-to-be. "Honey," he said, "I've been working on our budget. I want to spend some time going over it with you—and I think the honeymoon trip will give us a great opportunity to look at the numbers."

As Ecclesiastes 3:1 puts it, "There is a time for everything." The time for setting up a budget is not during your honeymoon.

STEP ONE: ESTIMATE YOUR LIVING EXPENSES

Every good budget begins with an estimation of how much money you need to live. To get a general idea of what you spend each year on everything from food and clothing to medical bills, gifts, and insurance premiums, use the Living Expense Inventory on page 60 to record your purchases over a one-month period. To get an idea of how to categorize your expenses, look ahead to the Budget Worksheet on page 63. Baby-sitters, cable television, and club or activity dues, for example, would all be recorded on the Living Expense Inventory under "Entertainment/Recreation" costs.

Once you've listed all your expenses for a month (and you may need to make copies of the Living Expense Inventory or create your own ledger so you'll have room to record all your expenses), total each column. Then, multiply each total by 12 to get a rough idea of what your annual expenses will look like. Your expenses will vary from month to month: heating bills, for example, may mean that your housing costs are higher in the winter than in the summer, and irregular car repairs may cause fluctuations in your transportation budget. Don't worry about these aberrations; at this point, your aim is simply to get a general picture of your spending habits.

STEP TWO: ALLOCATE YOUR RESOURCES

Using the data from your Living Expense Inventory, you are ready to preset the amounts that you and your spouse are willing to spend in each budget category. While the amounts you set are a function of your individual values and priorities, you may find the Family Income Percentage Guide on page 62 helpful in establishing a few general parameters. Record the amount you want to spend in each category on the Budget Worksheet on page 63. (Feel free to add or delete budget categories to tailor this worksheet to your family's individual spending habits.)

LIVING EXPENSE INVENTORY (Record actual spending for one month.)

Housing	Food	Clothing	Transportation	Entertainment Recreation	Medical	Insurance	Children	Gifts/Special Occasions	Misc.

Monthly Total

x 12

A few hints may help: Use an average figure for your monthly utility bills, and figure on spending about five percent of your annual mortgage payments for home repairs and maintenance. If you have car payments, outstanding credit card bills, or other installment loans, set up a budget category for "debt repayment." (Once you get rid of this debt, the only debt that will be factored into your monthly living expense is your mortgage payment, which is recorded in the "housing" category.) Items such as furniture and appliances don't have a budget category; those purchases are made out of your "margin"— the extra money you are supposed to have left over each month when you budget correctly.

STEP THREE: IMPLEMENT A CASH CONTROL SYSTEM

Here's where the going can get tough. It's easy to say how much you *want* to spend each month, but actually *controlling* the flow is another matter!

The idea behind using a cash control system is to provide you and your spouse with an immediate awareness of how your actual spending stacks up to your planned spending limits. You can keep track of your expenses in several ways. The simplest idea is to use the envelope system, where you put a predetermined amount of money into various envelopes (one for groceries, one for gas, one for clothing, one for entertainment, etc.) each month and then stop spending when the envelopes are empty. Unfortunately, in today's environment, the envelope system is neither very convenient nor very safe.

Judy and I use three checkbook registers in place of envelopes. We have one primary register in which we record all the funds deposited into our checking account. In addition, each of us has our own ledger in which we record our individual expenses. I am responsible for things like mortgage, utility, and insurance payments, while Judy pays for items such as gifts, groceries, and clothing. You can divide expenses any way you want to, but in order for the checkbook system to work, each of you must have assigned areas of accountability.

Practically speaking, here's how our system works: Each month, I record all our deposits in the main checkbook register. Then, based on the amounts we have predetermined to spend in our respective

YOUR FAMILY INCOME PERCENTAGE GUIDE*

Gross Income	$25,000	$35,000	$45,000	$55,000	$65,000	$	%
Tithe	10%	10%	10%	10%	10%	____	____
Taxes	13%	19%	20%	21%	25%	____	____
Debt	0%	0%	0%	0%	0%	____	____
Total Priority Expenses	23%	29%	30%	31%	35%	____	____
Net Spendable Income	77%	71%	70%	69%	65%	____	____
Living Expenses							
Housing	29%	24%	21%	19%	17%	____	____
Food	9%	9%	8%	8%	7%	____	____
Clothing	4%	4%	4%	4%	4%	____	____
Transportation	12%	9%	8%	8%	7%	____	____
Ent./Rec.	4%	4%	4%	5%	5%	____	____
Medical	4%	3%	3%	3%	3%	____	____
Insurance	4%	4%	4%	3%	3%	____	____
Children	2%	2%	2%	2%	2%	____	____
Gifts	1%	1%	1%	1%	1%	____	____
Miscellaneous	4%	5%	7%	7%	7%	____	____
Total Living Expenses	73%	65%	62%	60%	56%	____	____
Margin	4%	6%	8%	9%	9%	____	____

Assumptions*

1. All percentages are of gross income.
2. Figures are based on a family of four and are provided as a guide only. Your personal circumstances may necessitate different allocations.
3. The tax percentages assume that the standard deduction is taken.
4. There is no consumer debt.
5. Margin can be used for other expenses (private educations, etc.)

Source: *Master Your Money* by Ron Blue

BUDGET WORKSHEET

YEAR: _____

Amount We Will Budget   Amount We Will Budget

HOUSING

Mortgage/rent _____

Insurance _____

Property taxes _____

Electricity _____

Heating _____

Water _____

Sanitation _____

Telephone _____

Cleaning _____

Repairs/maintenance _____

Improvements _____

Furnishings _____

Supplies _____

Other _____

_____

Total Housing _____

FOOD _____

CLOTHING _____

_____

Total Clothing _____

TRANSPORTATION _____

Insurance _____

Gas & oil _____

Repairs/maintenance _____

Parking _____

Mass transit or commute _____

Other _____

_____

Total Transportation _____

MEDICAL EXPENSES

Insurance _____

Doctors _____

Dentist _____

Drugs _____

Other _____

Total Medical Expenses _____

INSURANCE

Disability _____

Other _____

_____

Total Insurance _____

CHILDREN

School Lunches _____

Allowances _____

Tuition _____

Lessons _____

Other _____

_____

Total Children _____

GIFTS/SPECIAL OCCASIONS

Christmas _____

Birthdays _____

Anniversary _____

Holidays other than

  Christmas _____

Other _____

Total Gifts _____

ENTERTAINMENT/RECREATION		MISCELLANEOUS	
Eating out	_____	Toiletries	_____
Baby-sitters	_____	Husband: lunches, etc.	_____
Magazines/newspapers/cable	_____	Dry cleaning/ laundry	_____
Vacation	_____	Animal care	_____
Clubs/activities	_____	Beauty/barber	_____
Classes/courses	_____	Other	_____
Other	_____		_____
Total Entertainment	_____	**Total Miscellaneous**	_____

TOTAL LIVING EXPENSES   _____

areas of responsibility, I allocate funds from the main ledger and record them as deposits into our individual ledgers. (I might, for example, put an $800 deposit into Judy's register, knowing that she will spend about that much on groceries, gifts, clothing, and the several other budget categories she handles.) Once a month, I reconcile our bank statement with our individual ledgers, and ensure that the amount we have left matches the balance in our main checkbook register. The whole process takes less than a half hour per month.

Research shows that simply using a credit card for the sake of convenience can make you spend at least thirty percent more than you otherwise would!

We also, as I mentioned earlier, use the data from our checkbook registers to keep track of our overall spending via a computer program. If you have a home computer, you might want to purchase a budget software program, which is often more convenient and accurate than paper-and-pencil record keeping. But no matter what sort of system you use to control your cash flow, *remember to limit your credit card use*. Research shows that simply using a credit card for the sake of convenience can make you spend at least thirty percent more than you otherwise would! Nothing can derail a spending plan faster than having to meet unexpected debt payments.

You will, however, have some unexpected expenses. Medical bills, car repairs, and other emergency needs can all put a strain on your spending plan. So can onetime expenses, like an annual family vacation. Plan ahead to absorb these budget busters by keeping the funds you don't spend during any given month in a savings account. This cash margin will enable you to meet unforeseen or irregular expenses without destroying your budget.

Finally, be flexible. There will be times when you may need to use funds allocated for one purpose for something else. Maybe you want to put your entertainment money toward the purchase of some new clothes. That's fine—as long as the switch is made intentionally and not behind your spouse's back.

STEP FOUR: EVALUATE AND REVISE YOUR PLAN

After you become comfortable with your cash-control system, you will need to evaluate and revise your spending plan periodically. Ask yourself these questions:

1. Are we staying within our allotted monthly spending levels? If not, why not?
2. Is our cash-flow margin accumulating as we expected? Are these savings reflected in our bank account balance?
3. Do we make our spending decisions with our short- and long-term goals in mind?
4. Is our net worth (the amount we own less the amount we owe) increasing?
5. Have our insurance needs changed?

In the last chapter we told you how our planning weekends have changed our lives. Your financial review should be part of these weekends. If you have not already done so, pull out your calendars and set a date for a planning retreat. As you go over your spending plan, keep your goals in front of you. Have they changed? Are you making progress toward achieving them? Does your spending plan need to be adjusted to allow you to accelerate your pace in terms of saving money for the future? Do you need to scale back to revise some overly ambitious goals, or to allow for a change in your circumstances—such as the birth of another child, a job change, or an unexpected medical need?

By focusing on your goals, you can use your spending plan to mark and measure your progress. Over time, your goals will change—and you can alter your spending plan accordingly. By using such a flexible and strategic approach to financial management, you won't find yourself looking at your sixty-first birthday and wishing you started saving earlier for retirement. Likewise, if your heart is set on building an addition for your family to enjoy, you will be able to plan to make your hopes a reality.

Remember, a spending plan is not a restrictive, inhibiting set of rules. Used properly, a spending plan is the cornerstone of financial harmony in marriage. And while it can't guarantee that you will live happily ever after, a strategically crafted budget will always reduce your potential for conflict. Not only that, but your budget—as unromantic as it sounds—is the secret to making your financial dreams come true.

Chapter Five

We're Being Eaten by the Borrow Constrictor

How to Conquer Debt Forever

---

*T*hat was a good workout. My arms are going to feel it tomorrow."

"Yeah," Chris agreed, grabbing a towel from his locker. He and Mike had been going to the gym three or four times a week for nearly two years, but Mike had not lost his initial enthusiasm. He liked nothing more than to push the limits of his endurance—and he often goaded Chris into doing the same.

"You seemed a little preoccupied today," Mike said, gazing at his friend. "Is everything okay?"

"Yeah," Chris said slowly, stuffing his sneakers into his gym bag. "Well, no. Not really. Carol and I aren't getting along too well."

"But I thought things were great. I mean, you got that great new house—she certainly seemed happy to show it off when Sharon and I came for dinner last week. Sharon would kill for a kitchen like that."

"Yeah, Carol likes the house. She's not too happy about the mortgage, but we'll be okay. Especially after I get my bonus check in a couple of months."

"So what is it? Doesn't she go for the sleeker, shapelier you?" Mike punched his friend's arm. "Maybe we need to get you one of those cool muscle T-shirts so she can better appreciate your biceps."

"Cut it out," Chris laughed. "This is serious. I bought her a pair of diamond earrings last week and she burst into tears. She won't even try them on—says they're too expensive."

"Wow. Can you get her to talk to Sharon? You know that ad on TV, the one about how diamonds are forever? Every time that comes on Sharon gives me the hairy eyeball. I'd love to get her something—but you know we can't afford it."

"Oh, come on, Mike. You make as much as I do. They let you buy the stuff with no money down, and then they give you a year to start paying it off. I've got twelve months before I even have to start thinking about how to pay for the earrings—and Carol could be wearing them right now for free!"

"You mean like she's driving that new minivan?"

"Exactly! Well, not exactly. We've already had to start paying on that one. And you want to talk about expensive? I could have gotten a BMW for what that thing is costing us! But hey—the kids love it. And I feel a lot better knowing that Carol's not carting everybody around in that old station wagon. That thing looked like it was about to blow up."

"I know what you mean. Our wagon just passed the 100,000 mile mark. But I'm hoping she still has a year or two left in her. And Sharon's not complaining."

"No? Well, count your blessings. I wish I knew what was bugging Carol. Maybe I ought to get her a new washing machine. You have to use a screwdriver to get ours to start."

"A washing machine? You think that will fix things?"

"Well, it would certainly help with this smelly stuff!" Chris laughed, hoisting his gym bag over his shoulder. "But you're right. A washing machine is not very romantic. Maybe I should get her some flowers . . ."

Debt. Almost everybody has it, but nobody likes it. If so-called "money problems" are blamed for the breakup of so many marriages today, we'd be willing to bet that indebtedness is the chief culprit in the vast majority of these cases. Even the strongest marriages can begin to buckle under the pressure of consistently spending more than you earn.

> *Even the strongest marriages can begin to buckle under the pressure of consistently spending more than you earn.*

Unfortunately, most Americans are incredibly naive about debt. We have no idea how much we actually owe, much less do we understand the impact that our current obligations will have on our future earnings. Today, the average American carries a credit card balance of $5,800 on which he pays 18.3 percent interest, making for a cash outlay of $929.70 per year in interest charges alone. What these numbers mean is that the average person has to pay nearly $1,000 in interest each year—even before he or she can begin to pay down the actual debt. Instead of reading statistics like these as a wake-up call, we take a perverse comfort in the fact that we are not alone—that our neighbors are just as financially strung out as we are.

To their credit—and discomfort—women are generally more sensitive to the debt issue than men. Not long ago, I fielded questions on a radio program, all of which turned out to be about debt. (That's not overly remarkable; debt is almost always the runaway favorite topic on financial call-in shows.) The thing that surprised me was that 100 percent of the callers were women. Their stories were all different, but they shared a common desire to reduce or eliminate their debt load. Not one of them asked about "creative financing" or ways to use credit to take advantage of an investment opportunity or some other "great deal."

You wouldn't find that sort of debt aversion in a room full of men. I talk to people all the time who want to refinance their loans, defer their payments, or use credit to stay "one step ahead of the game." Most of these people are men.

I don't mean to sound sexist or stereotypical, and I realize that I am speaking in very broad terms. I think my generalizations may stem from what psychologists point to as our most basic human desires: As people, we want significance and security. Our impression is that, of the two, men tend to focus on significance, while women care slightly more about security.

I am reminded of a story I've shared before about how I watched a man finance the purchase of a Rolex watch, using the jewelry store's long-term payment plan to buy the timepiece. When pressed for a down payment, the fellow pulled out a credit card. To him, the watch represented power, position, and prestige—and he didn't care what it cost (or whether or not he could even afford it) to identify himself with those attributes. Other men may attach value to something else, such as the car they drive. The newer or more desirable the model, the more important they feel. Almost anything—from a high-paying job to a low golf handicap—can contribute to a man's sense of significance.

Women, it seems to us, generally long for the comfort of a secure and stable future. That's not to say that their plastic doesn't whip through the credit card machine plenty fast; as any marketing professional knows, women do more than their fair share of spending the family dollars. The difference lies in how they feel when the bills arrive. Too many bills threaten a woman's sense of security—striking her at her most painful and vulnerable point.

For men and women alike, debt creates bondage.

I won't pretend to be a psychologist, or that I could even begin to understand why we behave the way we do. But after more than thirty years as a professional financial advisor, I know one thing for certain: For men and women alike, debt creates bondage. It dictates how you will spend the money you make in the months and years to come, it reduces your flexibility to take advantage of various opportunities that come your way, and it almost always puts an emotional strain on any relationship in which it appears.

COMMIT YOURSELF TO FREEDOM

Knowing the negative ramifications that debt can have, particularly on a marriage relationship, I decided to address the topic during a Promise Keepers event I spoke at last year. Studies show that Christians carry just as much debt as everyone else, so I felt fairly confident as to what would happen when I posed my question to the crowd.

"How many of you are in debt?"

Surrounded by a stadium filled with seventy thousand men, I watched as nearly every hand in the place went up.

"How many of you will commit to getting out of debt?"

A few hands dropped, but the overwhelming majority of the men were still with me.

"The average American family has $12,500 worth of consumer debt," I said. "That's not counting your home mortgages. And that means that, in this stadium alone, we've got $900 million worth of unpaid bills to meet. At 18 percent, the interest alone is costing us $200 million a year!"

I knew that I had the crowd's attention, and I pressed on: "That $200 million a year translates into $1 billion dollars in just five years—money that could be freed up to care for our families, our communities, and God's kingdom here on earth." Gazing out at the sea of faces, I asked for a commitment. "If you are willing to commit to get out of debt and move into a life of freedom, please stand with me now."

To say that the scene was incredible would be an understatement. I stood on the stage, looking around as nearly 70,000 men pledged themselves to destroy debt's hold on their lives. Financially, the potential impact of their decision was phenomenal. Even more significant was the way that their commitment—if they took it seriously—would affect their marriages.

I have repeated this challenge at other Promise Keeper gatherings, walking the men through the same four steps I am about to outline for you. As you read, remember that getting out of debt is rarely easy. But it is never impossible.

FOUR STEPS TO A DEBT-FREE MARRIAGE

Step One: Figure Out What You Owe

The first step in getting out of debt is to recognize how much you owe. Use the following worksheet to list your obligations, recording any money you owe to anyone for anything. The only debt you should exclude is your mortgage payment, since that obligation counts as a living expense in your monthly budget.

Step Two: Determine What Caused the Debt

Debt, in and of itself, is not always a problem. The Bible does not *forbid* borrowing; instead, Scripture repeatedly warns us about the dangers of *indebtedness*—chiefly, again, that debt creates bondage. As Proverbs 22:7 puts it, "The borrower is servant to the lender."

HOW MUCH DO WE OWE?

Creditor	Balance Due	Interest Rate	Payment Schedule Per Month	Until When
1.	$ _____	_____%	$ _____	_____
2.	$ _____	_____%	$ _____	_____
3.	$ _____	_____%	$ _____	_____
4.	$ _____	_____%	$ _____	_____
5.	$ _____	_____%	$ _____	_____
6.	$ _____	_____%	$ _____	_____
7.	$ _____	_____%	$ _____	_____
8.	$ _____	_____%	$ _____	_____
Totals	$ _____		$ _____	_____

There may be times in your life when you may have to borrow money, such as when you take out a loan to buy a home, launch a business, or fund a college education. In each of these cases, though, the benefits you receive will outweigh the costs involved, and you will have (or you *should* have) a realistic plan for repaying the loan on time. Knowing how and when you plan to get out of debt can greatly reduce the emotional weight of your obligations.

But what about *impulse* debt—the kind of indebtedness that results when we buy things we have neither the budget nor the plan to pay for? One of the most powerful delusions of debt is that buying something—a new outfit, some new furniture, a new car—will somehow make us feel good. I can't tell you how many husbands I know who, sensing trouble in their marriage, have tried to "fix" the problem by spending money on their wives. Like Chris, the fellow whose story you read at the start of this chapter, they buy everything from bigger houses to expensive jewelry in the mistaken hope that the purchase will satisfy their wives and improve their marriages. But in reality, just the opposite occurs! As the root problem—whatever it is—goes unaddressed, the pressure created by debt only adds new barriers to the relationship.

As you review the debts you listed in step one, think about why you spent the money in the first place. Borrowing money to buy your wife a car because her old one was unsafe or beyond repair is different than borrowing money to buy her a car that will look better in the carpool line or the office parking lot. Be honest with yourselves. Weigh your motivations—and then *take the steps necessary to address whatever root problems you discover.* Don't keep throwing money at a problem in hopes that it will go away; instead, resolve to stop using credit to pay for things you don't need or can't afford.

> *If you are going to take on debt, you need to have more than just a hope that you will pay back the money. You need to have a plan*

Step Three: Establish a Realistic Repayment Plan

Again, the Bible does not prohibit debt. It does say, in Psalm 37:21, that "the wicked borrow and do not repay." If you are going to take on debt, you need to have more than just a hope that you will pay back the money. You need to have a plan. If you don't have a plan, you need to get one.

Earlier in this chapter I said that getting out of debt is neither easy nor impossible. Look at the list of debts you drafted in step one. In order to get out from under that pile, you can do one of two things: You can increase your income, or you can reduce your expenses. For most people, it's easier to do the latter.

We all have "luxuries." We eat lunch at a restaurant instead of bringing a sack from home. We buy new shoes when our old ones could simply be resoled. We hire baby-sitters, grass-cutters, house-cleaners, car-washers, and hair-cutters when we could, in most cases, do the job ourselves. And I'm not talking about major purchases: by saving just $2.74 per day, you can add $1,000 a year to your budget. Ask God for wisdom and guidance as you look for creative ways to reduce your expenses.

Apply these savings to your debt pile, starting with the smallest obligation. By experiencing early success, you can motivate yourself to tackle successive hurdles. Focus your attack on the debts with the highest interest rates. Consider taking out a consolidation or home equity loan to obtain a lower rate—but watch out! If you use the funds from one of these loans to pay off your credit cards, don't make the mistake of using the cards again. Destroy them if you have to; the last thing you want is new debt to add to the old.

Finally, give yourself time. Jumping into a pit is always easier than climbing back out, and getting out of debt isn't something that happens overnight. But if you have a plan, and if you stick to it, you *will* get the job done.

Step Four: Be Accountable to Someone

Students are accountable to their teachers, athletes are accountable to their coaches, and employees are accountable to their bosses. No matter what task you have to perform, accountability builds focus and discipline into the equation.

To stay on track with your repayment plan, hold yourself accountable to someone whose judgment and integrity you trust. Don't turn to your spouse; this job could get ugly if the person has to hold your feet to the fire. Perhaps your pastor or an elder in your church would be willing to help. Another resource to consider is Larry Burkett's Christian Financial Concepts, a ministry dedicated to helping people better manage their financial resources. That telephone number is 1–800–722–1976.

Many people have also obtained help from the Consumer Credit Counseling Service, which you may reach at 1–800–388–CCCS. For a small monthly fee, the CCCS will help you develop a debt repayment plan and negotiate with your creditors to obtain lower monthly payments and reduced interest rates. But be forewarned: They may also ask you to turn over your monthly paychecks so they can decide which creditor to pay, and how much. Don't give them this authority except as a *very* last resort.

Husbands, I want to close this chapter with a word written specifically for you. If you love your wife, do whatever you have to do to get your family out of debt. Several years ago, I wrote a book about dealing with debt. It's called *Taming the Money Monster*. Debt is a monster, and it has a mean bite. You might not feel its teeth right now, but I'd be willing to bet that your wife knows they're there.

Getting out of debt comes with a multitude of built-in rewards. Not only will it help tear down the barriers that threaten your marriage, but it will strengthen your financial position and give you flexibility for the future. Once you get out from under the shadow of the debt monster, you can take advantage of financial opportunities as they arise and put your income to good use through strategic investing. Which brings us to chapter six . . .

Chapter Six

"Honey, I've Shrunk Our Portfolio!"

Choosing Investments You Can Live With

"Okay, we're going to do it," Rick said into the telephone mouthpiece, averting his eyes so he wouldn't have to meet his wife's gaze.

Becky stared at her husband in disbelief. Rick had just told their stockbroker to put a margin on a particular stock—an investment move which, if it worked, would generate huge rewards. If the plan backfired, though, and the stock did not perform as expected, Rick and Becky stood to lose a significant amount of money. Becky knew that Rick was an educated and informed investor, but this move represented an unnerving amount of risk. Not only that, but it appeared just plain foolish, since it meant placing almost all of their investment eggs in one uncertain basket.

"You can't do that!" she cried. "What about our agreement?"

Rick's mind raced back to the pledge he and Becky had made to each other several months ago. Their investment portfolio had been performing well—for which they were grateful to God—and they had agreed not to make any changes to the mix or process any financial transactions unless they were united in the decision. As a built-in accountability measure, they had confided their intentions to their stockbroker, Phil, a trusted friend who shared their Christian convictions.

"Honey, the numbers add up. This is an incredible opportunity. Phil thinks so, too—don't you, Phil?"

Becky could hear Phil's voice through the telephone line, but it didn't bring her any comfort. Vivid memories of the last time they had made a similar move flooded her mind. When that investment soured, it had been nothing more than a hiccup in their portfolio's growth, yet it had taught them a powerful lesson. "That was a warning," they had agreed, *vowing never to repeat their mistake by presuming on the future. Now, though, Rick was breaking that vow.*

"I can't believe you are doing this," Becky said, her voice hard. "I wash my hands of this—I am completely against it."

Rick hung up the phone, visions of future profits dancing in his head. Becky would come around—of that, he felt confident. The stock they were betting on had an incredible track record, and if things went as he and Phil had planned, Rick would be able to quit his job and pursue his dream of working with the poor or on the mission field. He wasn't greedy, just practical. Why couldn't Becky see that?

All Becky saw was the violation of her trust. Here was the man she had been married to for eleven years, acting like someone she hardly knew. Never before had he let her down. "You've fallen off the white horse," she said, turning her back on Rick and walking out of the room.

Weeks passed. The once brilliant stock began to lose its luster, gasping and sputtering with incremental drops in value. "I think we need to sell," Rick told Phil.

"Don't worry about it," the stockbroker replied, confident that the stock was still a winner.

Even so, Rick grew concerned. He wanted to talk things over with Becky. She could read an earnings report as well as he could, and he valued her advice. After all, their financial future was on the line. But Becky refused to discuss the stock. Rick had not listened to her, and she carried the wounds from that broken trust.

Soon, though, it became apparent to them both that the stock was in a free fall. As the price dropped, Rick and Becky watched as all their previous gains disappeared. Eventually the losses began to eat into their principal—the money that they had originally invested. Aware that they stood to lose the value of their entire portfolio, Becky stepped in and asked Phil to sell the stocks they had earmarked for their children's education. "Okay," Phil said, agreeing to sell some of the stock. "But really, you should hang in there. This stock is going to turn around."

A few months later, the stock went belly up. Rick was devastated. They had lost almost everything—including their dreams.

"I am so sorry," he confessed to Becky. "I got so wrapped up in that stock—I broke all the smart investing rules, and I should have known better. I was just too emotionally involved. All that money—"

"It's not about the money," Becky interrupted. "It's about trust. I don't care about the money—and I can forgive you. But I just don't know if I will ever be able to trust you with our money again."

In the last chapter we saw how debt can create bondage and erect barriers in a marriage relationship. Investing can be just as dangerous to healthy communication. It took several years to fully mend Becky and Rick's relationship. Rick refused to invest anything for a year and a half. Even after he began investing again—this time with a conservative outlook and with a new respect for Becky's intuition—she held on to her broken trust. She forgave Rick and she loved him deeply, but even years later, when Rick's careful investing earned an incredible thirty-percent return, Becky's genuine admiration was tempered by her memories. As she had told her husband: It wasn't about the money. It was about trust.

Even without a painful experience like Rick and Becky's, it can be difficult for couples to maintain an atmosphere of trust and open communication about investing. Many husbands and wives simply do not discuss their investments. I am constantly amazed by the number of men I meet who approach investing with the idea that their wives won't understand the proposals, or that they are not interested in financial matters. Either that, or the guys keep quiet because they figure that if they tell their wives what they are planning to invest in, the women will nix the idea.

If you think I am making this up, I wish you could stand at the podium with me during some of my speaking engagements. If the audience is strictly male, generalizations such as those I've just made elicit guilty laughter, knowing looks, and nods of understanding. But if the audience includes women, the men sit rigidly in their chairs, wearing poker faces and even getting defensive. Men know how they think; they just don't want to admit it in front of their wives.

Although I didn't acknowledge it at the time, the way I handled our finances during the early years of our marriage generated major problems in our relationship. Simply put, Judy didn't trust me. She had no idea what I did with our money, or what my actions might mean for our future.

We've already told you how focused Judy was on raising our children. At first, the money or what I did with it didn't matter; Judy was just glad that I put food on the table. But when I started an accounting firm in Indiana, things began to change. As she tells it, the steady stream of papers I asked her to co-sign for the business began to make her uncomfortable. She didn't understand exactly what she was signing, and I never took the time to explain things.

All Judy knew was what she saw: We were making payments on the two new cars I had purchased, we still had my college loans to pay off, and we took on a significant amount of debt when I started the business. From a financial standpoint, Judy was scared—but what was even worse was her fear that if she questioned any of my decisions, I might leave her. Remember, neither of us knew the Lord then. The way Judy saw it, I loved the business more than I loved her.

Even after we became Christians, I failed to bring Judy into the financial loop. In 1977, I sold my Indiana accounting firm so we could go into full-time ministry. At the end of the year, I realized I had an unexpected tax problem: The proceeds from the business sale had boosted my income, and I hadn't planned for the tax consequences this increase would create. On the advice of a Christian financial planner, I invested in some apartment buildings and a gold mine—two of the myriad tax shelters that everyone seemed to be jumping into at the time.

When I mentioned the investments to Judy, she instantly spotted a problem. Designed to shelter income and provide tax-reduction benefits, the apartments and the gold mine had no real economic promise. As investments, the chances that either asset would grow in value or generate income were slim. To Judy (and, eventually, to the bulk of the financial community), investments like these didn't make much sense. Even so, she did nothing to try to change my mind. "I was past the point where I wanted to protest—much less fight—about money," she says.

I knew, of course, that investing in the apartments and the gold mine carried a measure of risk; every investment is "risky," to some degree. But in my mind, the risk was secondary to our perceived need for a tax shelter. Heedless of Judy's perspective or the risk the investments carried, I rationalized my decision. (As things turned out, we did not lose any money and we did reap some tax benefits. But, as Judy predicted, the investments themselves turned out to be economically worthless.)

Any investment can be rationalized—especially if you are a man. Men seem uniquely capable of attaching a "no risk" or "low risk" label to any financial move they want to make. Not long ago, I met with a couple who had a large amount of money to invest. They wanted to know where they could get a thirty- to fifty-percent return, saying they had heard of something called a "market neutral" investment.

There is no such thing as a "risk-free" investment.

Never having heard that term before, I was intrigued. "What is a market neutral investment?" I finally asked.

"One where there is no risk," the fellow answered—with a completely straight face. "If the market drops, market neutral investments are not affected."

I wanted to laugh, but I looked at his wife. She was as concerned as any investor I have ever seen. From what I could tell, her husband was the financial "expert" of the family, but he had missed a truth that she intuitively understood: There is no such thing as a "risk-free" investment.

So how do you find the right balance? How do you maximize your potential rewards while minimizing your exposure to risk? Whether you have a lot of money to invest or just a little, how do you find the opportunities that make the most sense for you? How do you choose wise investments?

CHOOSING INVESTMENTS THAT MAKE SENSE

People who sell investment products would often have us believe that investing is a complicated process, undertaken only by "experts" who decide what to buy or when to buy or sell based on some sophisticated formula. While it always pays to do your homework, the reality is that wise investing is, for the most part, a matter of choosing the right principles to follow. It's a matter of choosing the right investment philosophy.

All of us, whether knowingly or not, make philosophical, principle-driven decisions about investing. For example, you can take a short-term approach to investing or adopt a long-term perspective. Either way, you have made a choice. And when you violate an investment principle—whether consciously or not—you must be prepared to pay the cost.

At RBC and in our personal lives, our investment philosophy is rooted in a number of biblically based, time-tested principles. When these principles are expressed in terms of the choices they invoke, the decisions you will need to make look like this:

1.   Do I have a short- or long-term perspective?

If you take a short-term approach to investing, you decide that you (or your advisor) can accurately predict the direction of a particular investment, so that you can "time the market" and know when to buy or sell. An investor with a long-term perspective, on the other hand, admits that he or she does not know which way the market will go in the short-term, but that, given five or ten years, an investment or group of investments should perform in a particular way.

Biblical wisdom—as well as practical experience—supports the long-term view. Proverbs 6:6–8 points to the wise, hard-working ant: "It has no commander, no overseer or ruler, yet it stores its provisions in summer and gathers its food at harvest." Likewise, Proverbs 15:27 should be a warning to all the market-timers whose investment strategy is to make a fast buck: "A greedy man brings trouble to his family."

During the Asian financial crisis late in 1997, I often awoke at 5:00 A.M. to watch the business news to see what the Asian fallout might be on the U.S. markets. As it was, I was concerned about the global financial situation; had I operated under a short-term mentality, I would have been anxious to the point of panic.

The flip side of the panic mentality was evident in a man-on-the-street interview I watched on television during the crisis. The camera crew stuck their microphone in front of a well-dressed, obviously affluent woman in New York City. "Are you worried?" the reporter asked, after confirming that the woman had invested in the stock market.

"No."

"You just told us you invested heavily in the stock market," the reporter protested. "And you're *not* worried?"

"No," the woman smiled. "Actually, I think this is kind of fun."

"The market just saw its worst since October of 1987! Everybody's panicking. You call that *fun?*"

"Well, I feel sorry for the folks who are upset, but I'm thinking of buying more stocks. I remember the 1987 crash. I didn't sell then, and I'm not going to sell now. I give my investments time. Things will turn around again."

Not all investments increase in value all the time, and by putting your eggs in several different baskets, you can reduce your overall risk and increase your overall return.

The woman was right. In 1987, it took only three months for the market to climb back to its pre-crash level. Ten years later, in 1997, the rebound took only three days. The only real losers were those investors who sold their holdings in a short-term panic. Investing takes time and, as Proverbs 13:11 puts it, "He who gathers money little by little makes it grow."

2.   *Will I diversify or concentrate my investments?*

People generally accumulate a large amount of wealth by concentrating their assets in a single company. Microsoft's Bill Gates is a case in point. For the average investor, though, this approach carries an unacceptable level of risk. With all your investment eggs in one basket, you have no downside protection should that asset not perform the way you want it to. Rick and Becky learned this lesson the hard way.

Asset diversification—putting your money in several different types of investments—is the cornerstone of a sound investment strategy. Not all investments increase in value all the time, and by putting your eggs in several different baskets, you can reduce your overall risk and increase your overall return. As Ecclesiastes 11:1–2 says, "Cast your bread upon the waters, for after many days you will find it again. Give portions to seven, yes to eight, for you do not know what disaster may come upon the land."

In general, the more you can diversify, the better. Instead of owning one stock, buy shares in several companies. Instead of putting all your money into the market at once, stagger your investments over time. Instead of buying only stocks, bonds, or real estate, acquire a mix of assets to broaden the overall risk-tolerance of your portfolio. There are any number of ways you can create a diversified portfolio; we'll look at some specific strategies later in this chapter.

3. Will I manage my own portfolio or rely on a financial professional?

With all the discount brokers and on-line investment services available today, many investors opt to save the professional advisor fees and commissions and manage their own portfolios. If you want to try this approach, be sure that you have the time and the skills necessary to do the job. Similarly, you should evaluate your personal tolerance for risk: Can you stand great swings in the market, or do they make you too nervous? If you are apt to panic, get yourself a stockbroker or another professional advisor.

I work in a financial and investment planning firm, but Judy and I do not manage our own portfolio. We don't even know, at any given moment, exactly where our money is invested or what the value of our portfolio is. Instead, we regard the wisdom of Proverbs 15:22: "Plans fail for lack of counsel, but with many advisors they succeed." We depend on a number of financial professionals, including a variety of mutual fund managers. If one manager (or one fund) underperforms, the performance of the others will work to minimize the negative impact that the downturn might otherwise have had on our portfolio.

4. How will I pay my fees?

When you make an investment, you pay for the transaction in one of two ways: either with a percentage—anywhere from three to seven percent of the transaction—or through a fee, which is typically driven by the total value of your portfolio.

With a transaction-based approach, every time you buy or sell securities you pay your broker a percentage of the transaction. If you purchased securities worth $1,000, for example, you could expect to pay anywhere from $30 to $70 for the transaction.

With a fee-based approach (which is the approach we use and recommend), you pay an annual fee, usually equal to one to three percent of the amount you have invested. Once that fee is paid, it doesn't matter how often you (or your mutual fund manager) buy or sell securities; you will not incur additional processing costs.

> *There will always be another opportunity down the road, and we don't need to be in a rush to get rich.*

These principles—a long-term perspective, asset diversification, professional financial management, and a fee-based investment approach—form the cornerstone of our investment philosophy. But they are by no means all-inclusive. The Bible is full of wisdom that has direct application to investing and financial management. In addition to the principles we've already outlined, here are a few other pointers to keep in mind:

Count the cost. When you consider an investment, ask yourself why you want to do it. Is the risk you are taking worth it? What will change if the investment performs as you expect it to? What will happen if you lose your investment dollar? As Luke 14:28 says, "Suppose one of you wants to build a tower. Will he not first sit down and estimate the cost to see if he has enough money to complete it?"

Honor your spouse. Psalm 133:1 says, "How good and pleasant it is when brothers live together in unity." God gave you a built-in investment advisor when you got married. Listen to each other's counsel and don't make a move unless you are in agreement.

Don't make hasty investment decisions. In my profession, I hear about "great deals" and "golden opportunities" all the time. If there's one thing we've learned from this endless parade of ideas, it's that there will always be another opportunity down the road, and we don't need to be in a rush to get rich. I like the way Proverbs 23:4 puts it: "Do not wear yourself out to get rich; have the wisdom to show restraint."

Don't fall into the "binary trap." The binary trap centers on the question, Should I do this or not? It only gives you two alternatives. Instead of wondering whether or not to pursue a particular investment, broaden your perspective with a different question: What is the *best* use of these discretionary funds? Pray the prayer of Philippians 1:10, that you may be able to "discern what is best and may be pure and blameless until the day of Christ."

Don't presume upon the future. When you take on debt without a realistic repayment plan, you gamble on your future. Likewise, when you invest money that you cannot afford to lose, you presume upon the future. James 4:13–15 says, "Now listen, you who say, 'Today or tomorrow we will go to this or that city, spend a year there, carry on business and make money.' Why, you do not even know what will happen tomorrow. . . . Instead, you ought to say, 'If it is the Lord's will, we will live and do this or that.'"

Don't worry. If an investment causes you anxiety or generates tension in your marriage, sell it. Peace is more important than profit. In fact, worry violates the commandment Christ gave us in his Sermon on the Mount: "Do not worry, saying, 'What shall we eat?' or 'What shall we drink?' or 'What shall we wear?' For the pagans run after all these things, and your heavenly Father knows that you need them. . . . Therefore do not worry about tomorrow, for tomorrow will worry about itself" (Matthew 6:31–34).

THE WHAT, WHY, WHEN, AND HOW OF EFFECTIVE INVESTING

Once you understand the principles behind effective investing and develop a solid investment philosophy, you can begin to craft an investment strategy that is custom-tailored to your individual needs and goals. Such a strategy, shaped by common understanding and consent, can provide a framework of mutual trust through which you and your spouse can make investment decisions.

As you read this section, keep a paper and pencil handy. Developing your own investment strategy involves answering a series of questions to flesh out concepts such as your personal tolerance for risk, your individual goals and priorities, and your investment timeline. As you review the following material, jot down any questions, concerns, or "to-do" items you think of so you can discuss them with your spouse and your professional investment advisor.

WHAT TO BUY

What investments to buy—that is, what type of investments to buy—is inextricably linked with *why to buy*. Why do you want to invest? Accumulating wealth should not be an end in itself; instead, it should be a means to an end. Remember: Money is a tool. Take another look at the financial goals and priorities you listed earlier in this book. Investing for a secure retirement is different from investing to afford a new car or a bigger house. Similarly, a young couple who wants to fund their children's college education will choose different investments than an elderly widow who wants a steady source of income.

If you've not already done so, sit down with your spouse and list and quantify your top three financial goals. Define them according to how much money you will need and when you will need it, and take this information with you when you meet with your financial advisor.

	Goal	Money Required	By When
1.	_____	_____	_____
2.	_____	_____	_____
3.	_____	_____	_____

The specific investments you choose to help you meet these goals will depend, to a large degree, on factors such as your age, your temperament (how much risk can you handle?), your tax situation, and your debt load or other financial commitments. For do-it-yourself investors who want to accumulate wealth in order to meet future goals and commitments, I recommend three broad categories of investments:

Cash or Liquid Assets

Savings accounts, money market funds, and treasury bills are all examples of liquid assets. These investments can easily be converted to cash and carry very little risk that you will lose your investment principle. Money market funds—available through most banks and brokerage houses—have the added appeal of being run by professional money managers who use diversification techniques within the fund to achieve the highest return and the lowest risk. And, as with cash in a savings account, you have the freedom to take your money out of the fund if a better investment opportunity arises.

Professionally Managed Stock and Bond Investments

A mutual fund is a pooled fund of money from many investors which is handled by a professional money manager. Typically, the money manager invests in (1) stocks to achieve long-term growth in the fund, (2) high-yielding investments to provide income for the investor, or (3) a combination of growth and income funds to meet both objectives. Therein lies the chief advantage of investing in mutual funds: In addition to the professional management, asset diversification, and liquidity offered by this type of investment, mutual fund investing allows you to choose a fund that fits your specific financial goals or investment interests. Some funds, for example, include real-estate type investments, giving investors the opportunity to invest in real estate without sacrificing the liquidity afforded by a mutual fund.

If you are interested in learning more about mutual fund investing or finding out about specific mutual fund opportunities, we recommend a monthly investment newsletter called *Sound Mind Investing.* Whether you are a beginning investor or an experienced money manager, you will appreciate the objective insights and biblical perspective offered in this journal. Designed to help individual investors manage their own portfolios, *Sound Mind Investing* highlights specific investment opportunities readily available through companies such as Vanguard and Charles Schwaab. To request information, write to SMI, P.O. Box 22128-R, Louisville, KY, 40252–0128, or contact them at their web address: www.soundmindinvesting.com.

Real Estate Investments

Investing in real estate can allow you to diversify your assets and round out your investment portfolio. However, personally owned real estate—such as a rental property—can take a great deal of time and experience, and it carries a fairly high level of risk. It is also, obviously, a relatively illiquid asset. If you want to include real estate in your portfolio, talk to your investment advisor about public real estate partnerships, which you can buy into for as little as $1,000 to $5,000 and which offer the same objective as personally owned real estate: namely, growth.

At our firm, we manage over $1.5 billion for more than 3,500 individual investors. More important than the specific investments we choose are the principles we follow: We invest for the long term, we encourage asset diversification, we use professional money managers, and we keep investment costs down by choosing a fee-based approach, rather than paying a percentage on each transaction made.

WHEN TO INVEST

You don't have to have thousands or even hundreds of dollars in the bank before you start investing. You can begin right now. Pay off all your high interest debt—credit cards, car loans, and other obligations—before you even think about checking the newspaper to see how the stock market is doing. You'll get a guaranteed return of as much as 16 to 21 percent, and you won't have to incur any risk.

Next, keep one month's worth of living expenses in an interest bearing checking account and sock away three- to six-months' worth in a money market fund or savings account. These ready cash reserves will protect your budget from any unexpected expenses or emergencies—thereby allowing you to pursue your more "sophisticated" investments without worrying about how to make ends meet if your utility bill takes a sudden jump.

Finally, divide your investment objectives into short- and long-term needs. Save for major purchases such as cars, furniture, or the down payment on a house in money market funds, CDs and treasury bills, or mutual funds. Use these investment options as well as bonds, equities, and real estate to meet longer term goals such as retirement, college education, a vacation home, or increased charitable giving. Consider speculative investing—investing in precious metals or with venture capital, for example—only when you have met *all* of your short- and long-term goals.

HOW TO INVEST

At RBC, we tell our clients that diversification is the key ingredient in a sound investment strategy. Diversification can be accomplished in three ways: investing in different asset classes, investing in different assets within each class of assets, and investing over time.

To invest in different asset classes, consider dividing your assets among several investments. Money market funds, savings accounts, treasury bills, and bonds offer both earning power and purchasing power—that is, the investment principal generates income as it grows in value. Stocks provide long-term protection against inflation. Real estate typically gives you a hedge against inflation. And gold and silver can be valuable assets during a time of monetary collapse or political upheaval.

Investing in different assets within each class of assets is achieved, for example, by buying smaller amounts of ten stocks instead of a large amount of just one stock. Similarly, you could invest in several different real estate properties instead of just one major holding.

To diversify by investing over time, you can reinvest gains in your portfolio and/or practice dollar cost averaging. Dollar cost averaging is simply investing the same amount of money in a mutual fund or stock at regular intervals over a long period of time. As the market fluctuates, dollar cost averaging reduces your overall risk because (a) over time, the stock market generally trends up, and (b) you resist the temptation to take short-term gains or to panic if the market drops and sell your holdings prematurely.

In addition to diversification, one of the most important "how-tos" of strategic investing involves choosing a financial advisor. You want to work with a qualified professional who understands your personal goals, your individual tolerance for risk, and your investment timeline. Not only is choosing the right advisor important for economic reasons, but it is vital to your marriage relationship. You want an advisor you both feel comfortable working with, someone you both trust.

Above all, you want an advisor who is competent. All of us have heard stories of investors who turned to friends, business associates, or fellow church members for financial advice—only to lose their money to sour investments, poor management decisions, and even elaborate financial scams. Just because someone is a Christian does not mean that he or she has the financial expertise, training, and wisdom to help you manage your money effectively.

In the coming chapter, which focuses on estate planning, we'll explore the how-tos of selecting and working with a financial advisor. Having a financial advisor you respect and trust is important under any circumstances, but nowhere does this role take on more emotional significance than in estate planning, as you work to protect and provide for your spouse and your children.

Chapter Seven

Where There's a Wife There's a Will

Safeguarding Your Spouse's Future

Sharon placed her hands on the briefcase, fingering the locks gingerly, as though they might shock her. All she felt, though, was an overwhelming sense of loss. "Oh, David," she whispered, "I really need you."

Scarcely a week had passed since David's funeral. His death had come unexpectedly—at a time when they thought they had beaten the odds. After David's six-month bout with leukemia, his doctors had finally located a suitable bone marrow donor, and the transfer operation—a risky procedure—had been an unqualified success. Sharon and David rejoiced in God's goodness.

Then the headache came. When David complained about the pain, the doctors seemed unconcerned; headaches, they said, were not uncommon after bone marrow transplants. Still, they wanted to check things out, so Sharon and David had returned to the hospital. Three days later he was dead, the victim of chicken pox in his brain.

Sharon drove home a widow. Never had she anticipated this turn of events, not even when David struggled against the leukemia. Oh, he had tried to prepare her for the possibility of his death, talking her through their budget and their insurance policies, but Sharon hadn't wanted to listen. Talking about death seemed like it would seal David's fate; the last thing Sharon wanted to accept was some sort of "death warrant" on her husband.

Now, though, she wished she had listened more closely. She and David had taught classes in financial management at their church, and Sharon took comfort in the fact that they had stayed out of debt, tithed regularly, and managed to raise their family without any significant financial trouble. But David was the planner, not her. He had had all the answers.

"I need help," Sharon had said during David's illness, staring at him through the thick sheet of hospital plastic that kept them apart.

"It will be okay," David reassured her. "If you get scared, just call Bruce."

Bruce. Sharon thought of their accountant, a man who, along with his wife, had become a trusted and faithful friend. Yes, she would call him, eventually. She knew she would need an advisor. Right now, though, she had to open this briefcase—the "toolbox" that held all their financial records and information.

Slowly, Sharon snapped the locks. Tears filled her eyes as she gazed at the contents. Insurance policies, contact names, legal documents, financial records—everything she would need was there, right down to the envelopes that had already been addressed and stamped for her to use.

"Oh, David, thank you," Sharon breathed. "You loved me before you left me."

Sharon closed her eyes, grateful to God—and to her husband, who had taken the time to leave a "love letter" of such powerful and inestimable worth.

Someone once said that your estate plan is the last message your family will ever get from you. In Sharon's case, the message in her husband's briefcase was an incredible testimony to his love and care for her. Unfortunately, Sharon's story is more the exception than the rule.

Your estate plan is the last message your family will ever get from you.

The average person spends forty or fifty years accumulating and preserving wealth—but less than *two hours* planning how those assets will eventually be distributed. Approximately seventy percent of us die without a will—and usually at a time other than we would have planned for or chosen. As the fire-and-brimstone preacher in the old movie *Pollyanna* forcefully reminds his congregation, "DEATH COMES UNEXPECTEDLY!"

Dying without a will creates problems for everybody, men and women alike. But of the two, women statistically have a lot more to worry about: Nine out of ten women outlive their husbands. And as a result of our collective aversion to will-making, there are many more widows walking around in Katherine's shoes than in Sharon's.

Katherine returned home one day to find her fifty-three-year-old husband dead on their living room floor. Because of his long-standing distrust of insurance agents, Katherine's husband had no life insurance. Neither did he leave a will or any sort of plan for his heirs to follow. As if her grief were not enough to contend with, Katherine found herself digging through cardboard boxes in their attic looking for documents she could not even identify! With a mortgage to pay off, three children to raise, and no source of income to rely on, Katherine came face-to-face with worry and fear.

No man who loved his wife—and, for that matter, no woman who loved her husband—would ever want to leave their spouse in such a precarious position. Yet it happens every day. People die without a will, usually for one or more of the following reasons: (1) an unwillingness to face or contemplate death, (2) an unwillingness to accept the financial cost of preparing a will, (3) an uncertainty about who to trust or how to go about drafting a will, or (4) a belief that their estate or property is too small to warrant any official estate planning documents.

In this chapter, Judy and I want to help you overcome these barriers. If you're looking to build mutual trust and intimacy into your marriage, developing an estate plan—as cold and unromantic as it sounds—is a sure-fire way to strengthen the foundation of your relationship. If you don't believe me, ask your spouse: "Honey, would you feel better if we had a will?"

While you're waiting for his or her answer, let me give you five more reasons why you ought to have a will:

1. As I mentioned earlier, a will is your last chance to send a message to your family. With a clear and professionally drafted will, your message can be one of love and provision. Without one, the very absence of any "last words" can generate fear, frustration, worry, and doubt.

2. You're going to need it. Thirty-six percent of us will die before we retire. You may not think of yourself as "old," but before you start brushing up on your golf game and making plans to visit your grandchildren, make sure that your estate documents are in order.

3. You can't control your assets from beyond the grave. If your plans for your wealth and your children are not clearly outlined in a

will, you forfeit any say you would otherwise have had in the matter. Without a will, the state will decide who gets your money. If you're a man, your wife will likely receive only one-third to one-half of whatever is left after the taxes and fees are paid; your children, parents, or siblings could wind up with the rest. If you're a woman and your husband remarries after you die, his new wife—and not your kids—could easily get the assets you left if he dies before she does. And there's a lot more than money at stake: Without a will, the state will decide who should raise your children and manage their inheritance for them.

4. Court charges, taxes, and other administrative fees can siphon off up to seventy percent of the value of your estate if there is no will in place. That figure looks all the more stark when you consider the flip side: According to estate planning attorney and author Zoe Hicks, "A good estate plan can dramatically reduce—and in most cases eliminate—estate taxes, professional fees, and other costs associated with the administration of an estate."[1]

5. Finally, providing for your heirs via an estate plan—including a will and life insurance—demonstrates obedience to God. Our scriptural mandate to care for our families is clear: "If anyone does not provide for his relatives, and especially for his immediate family, he has denied the faith and is worse than an unbeliever" (1 Timothy 5:8).

So there you have it: Six emotional, practical, financial, or spiritual reasons to get started on your estate plan. And since there's more to effective estate planning than simply drawing up a will, we will devote the balance of this chapter to the estate planning basics: choosing a financial advisor, getting your will in order, evaluating your insurance needs, and organizing your records.

CHOOSING AN ADVISOR

I remember talking with Judy about our estate plan. "I don't need to understand all the technical stuff and legalese," she told me. "I just need to know who to call—and I do." For Judy, the fact that she knows and trusts our financial advisor is all that matters. If anything should happen to me, she knows she can depend on Eric—a partner in our firm who acts as our personal financial advisor—to provide wise counsel and security for our family.

Do you have a financial advisor you know and trust? Most people spend more time and effort shopping for a computer or a microwave oven than they do a financial advisor. When it comes to finding financial help, many folks simply turn to the first stockbroker or insurance salesman they meet: generally it's the fellow who lives next door, or who sits behind them in church, or who has a kid on their daughter's soccer team. But just because someone *knows* you does not mean that he or she truly *understands* your needs—or, more importantly, that he or she has the experience and expertise necessary to give you professional, objective, and competent advice.

> *Most people spend more time and effort shopping for a computer or a microwave oven than they do a financial advisor.*

Choosing a financial advisor could be the most important estate planning decision you will ever make. Start your search by interviewing several prospective advisors. Many financial planners, attorneys, insurance agents, and other advisors offer complimentary consultations for potential clients. As you meet with these people, keep in mind that the more complex your estate is, the more you need to work with someone who has a strong tax and estate planning background. If, for example, your estate includes unusual tax issues, blended families, or other complicated circumstances, be sure that your advisor specializes in transfer taxes and probate laws and procedures.

Don't be afraid to ask questions about an advisor's technical expertise. What degrees or certifications does he or she hold? What is his or her investment track record? What sort of clients does he or she cater to? Most importantly, does the advisor's expertise pertain to your particular needs?

Similarly, you will want to find out about the advisor's estate planning philosophy. If planning from a biblical perspective is important to you, make sure that your advisor shares your values. When you are trying to decide things like how much money to leave your children or whether you want to set up a trust to benefit a favorite charity, an advisor who understands your needs and goals can make all the difference.

Finally, find out how the advisor is compensated. Financial planners are generally paid in three ways: fee only, commission only, or fee plus commissions. According to the Consumer Federation of America and the National Institute for Consumer Education, the majority of people offering financial advice "earn some or all of their income selling mutual funds, annuities, insurance, and other financial products to implement their recommendations." The problem with this setup, the organizations say, is that "advisors" who are also salespeople "inevitably face a conflict of interest and will almost certainly be tempted to steer clients into products in which they have a financial interest." Your best bet for objective and unbiased financial advice is to work with a "fee-only" financial planner—someone who is compensated solely by fees paid by their clients. Look for an advisor who charges either an hourly rate, a flat retainer fee, or a percentage of assets under management.

Above all else, choose a financial advisor you and your spouse both trust. At RBC, our client managers meet with both husbands and wives so as to establish relationships with both spouses. Since your financial advisor is apt to be working with only one of you in the future—and with the statistical likelihood of a wife surviving her husband—it is especially important for wives to feel comfortable with the advisor you select.

DRAFTING A WILL: SIX DECISIONS YOU NEED TO MAKE

Before you meet with a financial advisor or hire an attorney to draft your will, it's a good idea to think through some of the decisions you will have to make about how you want your estate to be distributed. Again, this is something you will want to work on together. I'll never forget the time I met with a well-meaning and generous-minded millionaire who had planned to leave all of his assets to charity. His wife had no idea of his net worth, much less of his plans for distributing their wealth. When I asked him how she would feel when she discovered the value of his estate and that she had had no part in determining where the millions would go, he realized his mistake.

One of the first decisions you need to make has to do with the management and administration of your estate. I generally advise people to name their spouse as their executor and trustee, recognizing that he or she can always hire a financial advisor to manage the estate's assets, if necessary. When you appoint a bank or a nonfamily member as your trustee or executor, control of the estate literally passes out of your family's hands when you die.

My book *Generous Living* offers more information on effective distribution of wealth via your estate, including advice on issues like how much to leave your children or deciding which charities you want to support. Your financial advisor can show you how to implement these decisions and minimize taxes using specific estate planning tools and techniques. In general, though, you should be prepared to answer six basic questions:

1.   How much do you want to leave your children?

While leaving your children financially set for life can be hazardous to their future work ethic as well as their self-esteem, you cannot neglect your God-given responsibility of providing for your heirs. The "how much" question is dependent, to a large degree, on factors such as your children's ages, specific needs, and ability to handle money wisely.

2.   How should you leave your assets?

To enable your family to pay any estate taxes owed to the IRS, at least some portion of your estate must be left in a relatively liquid form, such as cash or stocks that can be quickly sold. If you have young children, consider leaving the majority of your assets to them in a trust that will provide annual income for their support. Ask your financial advisor about various trusts and which ones make the most sense for you.

3.   How much should you leave to other family members and friends?

If you have family members, friends, or employees you want to provide for via your will, ask your financial advisor about the best ways to meet these objectives. For example, if your sister is a single mom, you might want to establish a trust that would provide extra income during her lifetime. When she dies, the remaining balance in the trust would go to a charity you designate.

4. How much do you want to leave to charity?

When you die, you will have the opportunity to give amounts of money that would have been impossible during your lifetime, either through the sale of your home, business, or other assets, or through life insurance proceeds. While the Bible does not specifically address giving through your estate, we advise our clients to consider giving a percentage of their estate to charity—both for tax reasons and as an acknowledgment of God's lordship in their lives, now and throughout eternity.

5. How do you want to leave assets to charity?

You can give money to charity either through an unrestricted gift (one with no strings attached) or via a restricted gift—one in which you designate how or when the money will be used. You can also give to charity via various trusts, which can be used to benefit your children now and the charity later, or vice versa. Ask your financial advisor about Charitable Remainder Trusts and Charitable Lead Trusts.

6. How much do you want to pay in taxes?

The obvious answer to this question is "as little as possible." Talk to your financial advisor about reducing the size of your taxable estate via irrevocable life insurance trusts, the annual gift exclusion, and charitable giving options. Under current tax law, and with proper planning, you can expect to pay *nothing* in estate taxes if the value of your estate is less than $1.25 million in 1998. (In 1999, the exclusion equivalent jumps to $1.3 million; after the year 2000, the exclusion amount increases gradually to $2 million in the year 2006 and beyond.)

ASSESSING YOUR INSURANCE NEEDS

Having a will is one of the ways you can fulfill your God-given responsibility to provide for your family. Life insurance is another.

Most people do not have enough life insurance—either because they think they can't afford it or they simply do not realize how much they need. Neither of these objections is a valid excuse for failing to provide adequately for your heirs. Anyone can get life insurance, and unless you have no family or support responsibilities, or your investments are substantial enough to generate all the income your family will need, getting life insurance should be a top financial priority.

In general, you need a life insurance policy equal to ten times your annual income.

You can buy life insurance in several forms: annual renewable term, traditional whole life, a hybrid policy (combining term and whole life), and universal life. Deciding which of these options makes the most sense depends on several factors, including how much insurance you need, how long you will need it, and how much you can afford.

To get a more specific idea of how much insurance you need, complete the following worksheet titled "How Much Life Insurance?" Then contact a well-established, reputable insurance company and discuss your options with an agent. *Term insurance* provides the most coverage for the lowest initial premiums, making it suitable for young families who don't always have the extra funds available for insurance. However, since term insurance premiums increase every year, it's a good idea to shift a part or all of your insurance dollars to a *whole life policy* as soon as you can afford the higher initial premiums.

Universal life, which combines the income-producing features of an investment with a term-type insurance policy, offers policy holders flexible premium payments and the ability to withdraw cash from the policy. However, since universal life combines products with two different objectives—investment income and insurance protection—you may not get the economic results you could by pursuing these objectives independently of one another. The one-stop-shopping of a universal life policy is convenient, but it does not always make sense from a financial standpoint.

HOW MUCH LIFE INSURANCE?

1. **Annual** living expenses of survivors (spouse, children, etc.)
   (Consider 70% of current family living expenses) $_____   (1)

2. Less: Expected **annual** benefits

   a. Social Security benefits $_____

   b. Survivor's pension benefits $_____

   c. Survivor's earned income $_____

   d. Other income $_____

   Total expected annual benefits $_____ (2)

3. Net living expense shortage (or surplus)
   (Line 1 minus line 2) $_____ (3)

4. Amount of capital required to produce living expenses shortage $_____ (4)
   (Line 3 dividied by projected rate of return of invested capital.
   Consider using a conservative return rate to adjust for inflation.)
   Inflation-adjusted Rate of Return _____%

5. Plus other lump-sum expenses

   a. Final expenses/estate costs $_____

   b. Mortgage cancellation $_____

   c. Education fund or other $_____

   d. Emergency fund $_____

   Total lump-sum expenses $_____ (5)

6. Total capital required (Line 4 plus Line 5) $_____ (6)

7. Less: Present capital

   a. Income producing assets $_____

   b. Present life insurance $_____

   Total Present Capital $_____ (7)

8. Amount of capital insurance to be added, if any
   (Line 6 minus Line 7) $_____ (8)

This worksheet is designed to provide an estimate of life insurance needs. Two families with identical situations may reasonably conclude that their insurance needs differ significantly.

PUTTING IT ALL TOGETHER: ORGANIZING YOUR ESTATE

It's not hard to imagine the sense of relief Sharon must have felt when she opened her husband's briefcase and found all the papers and information she needed to successfully navigate the weeks and months following her husband's death. Likewise, it's not difficult to grasp the frustration, fear, and anger that the other widow, Katherine, must have experienced as she sifted through attic boxes, looking for papers that might not even be there. The most carefully crafted estate plan can be rendered ineffectual when instructions or other important documents are missing in action.

Few organizations do a better job teaching people how to organize their estate than Crown Ministries. Headquartered in Longwood, Florida, Crown Ministries is a national organization that offers small group Bible studies and other tools designed to help people manage their finances according to scriptural principles. In the final pages of this chapter, Judy and I want to share one of the estate planning worksheets we have used, which are excerpted from the Crown Ministries curriculum. This information is not intended to fully organize your estate; rather, it covers the basics. For a more thorough treatment of estate planning and organization, please contact Crown Ministries at 888–972–7696 (or visit the organization's web site at www.crown.org) to obtain a copy of their excellent workbook, titled *Set Your House In Order*.

ORGANIZING YOUR ESTATE

Date:_____

WILL AND/OR TRUST

The Will (Trust) is located: _____

The person designated to carry out its provisions is:_____

If that person cannot or will not serve, the alternate is: _____

Lawyer:_____ (Phone) _____

Accountant: _____ (Phone) _____

INCOME BENEFITS

1. Company Benefits:

My/our heirs will begin receiving company benefits as follows: _____

_____

Contact: _____ (Phone) _____

2. Social Security Benefits:

To receive Social Security benefits, go in person to the Social Security office located at:

_____

This should be done promptly because a delay may void some of the benefits. When you go, take the following: (1) my Social Security card, (2) my death certificate, (3) your birth certificate, (4) our marriage certificate, (5) and birth certificates for each child.

3. Veteran's benefits:

You are/are not eligible for veterans' benefits: _____

To receive these benefits you should do the following: _____

4. Life insurance coverage:

Insurance company: _____ Policy #_____

Face Value: _____ Person Insured: _____ Beneficiary: _____

Insurance company: _____ Policy #_____

Face Value: _____ Person Insured: _____ Beneficiary: _____

Insurance company: _____ Policy #_____

Face Value: _____ Person Insured: _____ Beneficiary: _____

FAMILY INFORMATION

Family member's name:

_____Address: _____

Social Security # _____

_____Address: _____

Social Security # _____

_____Address: _____

Social Security # _____

_____Address: _____

Social Security # _____

_____Address: _____

Social Security # _____

_____Address: _____

Social Security # _____

MILITARY SERVICE HISTORY

Branch of Service: _____Service Number: _____

Length of service:_____From: _____ Until: _____

Rank: _____Location and description of important military documents:

_____

_____

FUNERAL INSTRUCTIONS

Funeral Home:_____ Address: _____

_____ Phone: _____

My/our place of burial is located at: _____

_____

You request burial in the following manner: _____

_____

You request that memorial gifts be given to the following church/organizations:

_____Address:_____

_____Address:_____

Source: © Crown Ministries Practical Applications Workbook

Chapter Eight

Leaving and Cleaving

Building a Marriage with No (Purse) Strings Attached

"The brick house on the corner just came on the market. Why don't you and Anna swing by there after dinner and check it out?" Helping himself to the mashed potatoes, Martin looked hopefully across the dinner table at his son, Trey.

"Dad," Trey said, "you know we can't afford a place like that."

"Ahh—but there's where you're wrong. Your mother and I have a little surprise for you, right, darling?"

Eloise smiled at her husband. "We would really like for you all to be close to us. I know the houses around here aren't cheap, but this is a wonderful neighborhood. It's safe, and it's the perfect spot to raise a family. Anna thinks so too, don't you, dear?"

Anna fingered her napkin, uncertain how to answer her mother-in-law. Something was up—of that much, she was sure. "Yes," she finally said, "it's a lovely neighborhood."

"Well, then, it's all settled!" Eloise looked triumphant. "Your father and I have already discussed this, and we want to give you the down payment for that home. I talked to the real estate agent this morning—she can show us the house tomorrow afternoon. Anna, darling, you can get away from the school by 3:00, can't you?"

"But Mom—" Trey started to interrupt.

"There will be no buts about it!" Eloise said, raising her hand for silence. "Look, we know you two want to start a family—the sooner the better, right? This way, the house will be all ready when Anna quits teaching. And we'll be right here to help you settle in." Eloise winked at Anna. "And I think you'll find that we charge far less than the other baby-sitters in town!"

"Dad—" Trey turned to his father. "Dad, this won't work."

"Don't you want our help, son?" Martin sounded hurt. "I would have thought you'd be grateful."

Trey realized that he stood a good chance of offending his parents. He knew they meant well, and that their offer was motivated by a genuine concern for his and Anna's well-being. But he also knew they couldn't accept the money. He looked at Anna for support, and seeing the encouragement in her eyes, he plunged ahead.

"Listen, Dad," Trey began. "We can't buy that house—or any other house around here, for that matter. We don't have the money—"

"But with the down payment—"

"That's just it," Trey continued. "You are willing to give us a down payment—and Anna and I truly appreciate your offer. But we'd be the ones paying the mortgage every month. Anna is hoping to quit her job when we have kids, and living on my income isn't going to put us in this neck of the woods any time soon."

Martin was silent, but Eloise wasn't ready to give in just yet. "What if we gave you just a teensy allowance every month—just something to help you get by for a while?"

Anna cringed. She knew that, despite her mother-in-law's good intentions, the "teensy allowance" would not come without a price. Eloise would perceive the money as an invitation to influence—or, more accurately, meddle in—the affairs of her children and, eventually, her grandchildren. Having secured her position, she would come through the door of their lives like a Sherman tank.

The irony of the situation, Anna realized, was that Martin and Eloise truly loved them. Their offer of financial help stemmed from a genuine desire to protect and care for their children. Having the means to be generous with their offspring, they saw no reason to hold back. As Anna wondered whether she should express her concerns, Trey's voice interrupted her thoughts.

"Mom, Dad—please. You cannot imagine how grateful Anna and I are for your love, and for all the ways you've supported us until now. Even just having us over for dinner like this is a real treat. But," Trey continued gently, "put yourself in my shoes. When I married Anna, I accepted the responsibility to care for her—physically, emotionally, and *financially. That's not a burden; it's a blessing. Please . . . allow me to do my job."*

Martin and Eloise were silent as they considered their son's words. Finally, Martin cleared his throat. "I understand," he said, slowly. "We would never want to take any blessing away from you. In fact"—Martin reached over and took Eloise's hand—"I think that's just the way we'd want it to be, if we were in your shoes."

Eloise smiled at her husband. "You're right, of course. But," she continued, turning her attention toward Trey and Anna, "I'm still planning to come baby-sit. I don't care how far away you live!"

When Judy and I got married, our folks were not in any position to help us financially. All they gave us was a baby bed and a high chair—and, in fact, I even had to buy Judy's father's old suits from her mother. Judy's dad had passed away right before we got married, and her mother sold me his suits so that I would have something to wear to my job interviews! Having worked my way through college with no expectation of financial support from my family, I did not count on—or receive—any sort of economic help from either of our parents.

Even so, when Judy and I heard about Trey and Anna, and how Trey had respectfully stood up to his parents, I couldn't help but wince. While I found it easy to "leave and cleave" as I got married and moved out of my parents' home, I hadn't counted on my mother's ability to manipulate us—specifically, me—from an emotional standpoint. Growing up, I had learned (along with my father) that keeping Mom happy was the secret to peace in the home. We would do just about anything to keep from crossing my mother. Thus, when Judy and I got married and Mom began to make her presence—and her opinions—known in our lives, I did nothing to stop her advances. To me, the habitual pattern of catering to my mother was more important than protecting Judy or meeting her needs.

Looking back, I realize how wrong I was and how much my passivity hurt Judy—as well as our relationship. When God formed Eve out of Adam's flesh and bones, he established the model for marriage:

"A man will leave his father and mother and be united to his wife, and they will become one flesh" (Genesis 2:24). This pattern makes sense; yet for a young man or woman, leaving home to start a new life with another person can be an intimidating experience. No matter what your upbringing was like—no matter how good or bad your family relationships were—the life you leave behind is a comfortable one, if only by the fact of its familiarity. Moving into uncharted territory with only your spouse to cling to is, for many young couples, a challenge.

For parents, too, the leaving and cleaving process can present a daunting experience. Even when they are genuinely thrilled with their child's choice of a marriage partner, letting go is a bittersweet sensation. As author Jeanne Hendricks told us not long ago, "You pour your life into a person for twenty or twenty-five years, and then someone else gets the benefit of all your hard work!"

In the past seven years, Judy and I have "let go" of our three daughters, the oldest of our five children. While there is always an element of uncertainty in watching a daughter leave home, we are grateful for the good marriages our girls have. The challenge for us, as for so many parents, is to successfully walk the line between being meddlesome and helpful, between loving our kids and creating in them an unhealthy dependency on us.

Unlike our parents, Judy and I are in a position to be able to help our children financially. As we consider the appropriateness of giving them money or other material gifts, we have developed an informal set of guidelines which help determine our behavior:

First, our children know that, while we will always be available to love and support them, they should not count on us to "bail them out" of difficult financial situations, particularly if the trouble arises from unwise decisions or foolish behavior.

Next, Judy and I are happy to give financial gifts to our children, but we do not feel obliged to treat all five of them equally. We do not discuss the money or other gifts we give to one child with the others, and (we assume) they do not talk about them, either.

Finally, when we give something—particularly money—to any of our children, we do so with no strings attached. We understand (and our children recognize) that our gifts are not designed to influence their attitudes or behavior.

Judy and I feel blessed to be able to share what we have with our children, especially when we consider that our own parents did not have this opportunity. Even so, we have been careful to define the balance between sharing with our kids and making them dependent on us, either financially or emotionally. One of the best "litmus tests" we have found to help us strike the right balance is to look at our children's character. Even when they were growing up, and we had to consider the wisdom of spending money on things like new clothes, tennis lessons, or private school, we paid careful attention to how our choices affected their character. Did our children demonstrate self-discipline and responsibility? Were they able to make wise, independent decisions? Did they exhibit a respect for authority and a willingness to take care of their belongings? Most important, were they grateful for the financial blessings and opportunities we gave them? If we ever detected a demanding or expectant attitude, we knew we had crossed the line between giving "enough" and "too much."

> *When we give something— particularly money—to any of our children, we do so with no strings attached.*

DANGEROUS GENEROSITY

As we have watched many of our friends and clients walk this difficult line, Judy and I have seen, firsthand, the danger that economic assistance can pose, particularly to young couples as they struggle to adjust to new family roles and relationships. Many of the threats we have witnessed are statistically charted and recorded in the intriguing book *The Millionaire Next Door*. In this book, authors Thomas J. Stanley and William D. Danko make a convincing case against what they call "economic outpatient care": the "substantial economic gifts and 'acts of kindness' some parents give their adult children and grandchildren."[1]

According to Stanley and Danko, the more dollars adult children receive, the fewer they accumulate. Those who are given less money accumulate more. Why? As Stanley and Danko explain it, it is much easier to spend other people's money than money you make yourself.

Stanley and Danko's research points to several reasons why recipients of economic outpatient care wind up as underachievers in generating income. For starters, adult children who receive gifts tend to consume more and invest less than their non-receiving neighbors. It's the old "if-you-give-a-mouse-a-cookie" story. Just as the mouse will ask for a glass of milk, then a napkin, and so on, so getting an expensive rug can create a perceived need for nicer furniture, curtains, and lamps. With this increased spending/consumption level, there simply isn't as much room in the budget for savings and investing.

Another problem stems from the perception of who actually owns the resources. An adult child who is the frequent recipient of financial aid may come to see his parents' assets as his own. As time passes, he may begin to count on the security those assets represent—and even resent his parents for any spending or giving decisions they make that do not relate to him.

A third factor which limits an adult child's ability to build wealth is the high dependence on credit that typically marks people who receive periodic gifts of cash or other assets. If a hoped-for windfall from his parents does not arrive on time, the gift receiver is apt to use credit to support his or her consumptive lifestyle. After all, they figure, a sizable inheritance will eventually be coming their way.

In addition to the problems pinpointed by Stanley and Danko—the inability to save or invest, the misconceptions about asset ownership, and the high dependence on credit—there are other significant dangers associated with parental generosity. A crippled ability to reach financial independence is just the tip of the iceberg. Other problems—those related to issues of character and emotional stability—lurk just below the surface.

FINANCIAL SUBSIDIES: THE CHARACTER TORPEDOES

Luke 15:11–31 tells the story of the Prodigal Son, the young man who asked for—and got—an early inheritance from his father. With no work ethic to draw on, no ability to delay gratification, and no understanding of the concept of limited resources, the boy was doomed. He squandered the money and was forced to live in a pigsty before he finally humbled himself and went home to ask his father's forgiveness.

Suppose this young man had set out to see the world with a new bride in tow. Could their marriage have withstood the pressure? Never having worked outside his father's home, the fellow didn't have much of a resumé. In fact, the only job he could get was as a pig feeder. To say that this career path would not impress his young bride would be an understatement. Could the boy's self-esteem survive her doubts?

And what of their inability to delay gratification? The son had already demonstrated an unwillingness to put his desires on hold; that much was clear from the moment he prematurely demanded his share of the inheritance. Would the young couple have the discipline they needed to cut back on their living expenses, making lifestyle sacrifices in order to save a portion of the pig-feeding paycheck?

A low sense of self-esteem, a reduced or nonexistent work ethic, an impaired ability to delay gratification, and an ignorance about financial realities are the often inevitable character defects found in children whose parents establish a pattern of subsidizing their income.

Finally, would they even recognize their plight? Never having been exposed to the concept of limited resources—and the fact that you cannot have everything you want—they might continue in their consumptive lifestyle, oblivious to the unpaid bills that threatened their security. Eventually, the wife might wonder at (and even resent) her husband's inability to meet her needs. With a growing sense of frustration and disappointment, she might be tempted to look elsewhere to find material satisfaction. Another man? Perhaps. Her parents? Maybe. But if they agreed to send her some money on the next camel train, chances are that it would only further depress their son-in-law's sense of self-worth and drive a wider wedge into the already fragile marriage relationship.

A low sense of self-esteem, a reduced or nonexistent work ethic, an impaired ability to delay gratification, and an ignorance about financial realities (no, you can't always get what you want) are the often inevitable character defects found in children whose parents establish a pattern of subsidizing their income. Of equal concern is the more obvious problem when such gifts come with strings

How do you cut the economic bonds without severing your family ties?

attached. Anna, the young wife whose story we recounted at the outset of this chapter, told us that, despite her mother-in-law's generous nature, there would undoubtedly be consequences to consider. Having paved the way for her children to purchase a home, Eloise would want a say in everything from how it was decorated to which social clubs and neighborhood organizations Trey and Anna did—or didn't—join. And when the grandchildren came along, what would stop Martin and Eloise from showering them with money or gifts? Even special outings—normally a welcome aspect of family life—could serve to strengthen the grandparents' hold on their grandchildren's lives and perpetuate the cycle of dependency.

Looking down the road, perhaps the most sobering issue of all is this: What happens when one or both of the gift-givers dies? The dependency cycle may break—but that won't solve any problems. Without the financial fortitude and discipline to "make it" without his or her parents' help, an adult child's future prospects are grim. An inheritance may soften the blow, but without an ability to show restraint and invest the money, it won't last forever.

CUTTING THE PURSE STRINGS WITHOUT SEVERING THE FAMILY TIES

At this point, if you are a parent, you may be rethinking any notions you have held about loving your children with your wallet. If you're an adult child of such a generous-minded parent, you may be rethinking your willingness to accept such a demonstration of love. In either case, though, you probably do not want to offend your loved ones. So how do you cut the economic bonds without severing your family ties?

Before we answer that, Judy and I want to clarify something. We are not advocating a wholesale rejection of all family gift-giving and receiving. On the contrary, the professional advisors in our firm often counsel clients to give cash, stocks, and other assets to their children and grandchildren as a tax-wise strategy for reducing the overall size of their estate. Likewise, many of our clients frequently pay for things like family vacations. By allowing his in-laws to pay for his family to fly home for Christmas, one doctor we know was able to enjoy a warm family reunion and still have funds available to meet his annual charitable giving goals.

And according to *The Millionaire Next Door*, many of today's millionaires received college tuition assistance from their parents. Grateful for the advantages their education provided, the millionaires now spend a large amount of their own resources on education for their children and grandchildren—much more than they would ever consider spending to help their kids buy a home or meet mortgage payments.[2]

Giving, then, is not necessarily a problem. In fact, the Bible is full of examples of God's generosity toward his children. Financial blessings, the gift of children, protection from danger, eternal rewards, even salvation—all these and more are evidence of God's love for us. I love the way John acknowledges God's goodness in 1 John 3:1: "How great is the love the Father has lavished on us, that we should be called children of God!"

A WORD TO PARENTS . . .

Parents naturally want to give good things to their children. That's fine. The trouble starts when the gifts become part of a cycle of dependency and expectation, and when the "economic outpatient care" is used to fuel a consumptive, undisciplined lifestyle.

So how can we avoid that trap? What sort of gifts can we give our children that won't set them up for financial failure or prove damaging to their character? One commonsense answer is to think long-term. Before making any gift, ask yourself several questions: Is my son or daughter financially mature enough to handle this asset? Could it hurt his or her marriage relationship? If we help them buy this house (or this furniture, country club membership, car, etc.), will it contribute to a life of consumption and open the door to even greater financial "needs" and desires?

Then, too, you need to check your motives. Can you give a gift with no strings attached? Or, are you subtly positioning yourself to gain a measure of influence or control over your children's lives? Be honest with yourself about why you want to help your children and what you expect the results of your economic assistance to look like.

Stanley and Danko advise their readers to "teach your children to fish." They place a high premium on educational opportunities, encouraging parents to create an "environment that honors independent thoughts and deeds, cherishes individual achievements, and rewards responsibility and leadership."[3] They also offer three words of wisdom to the would-be wealthy: FRUGAL, FRUGAL, FRUGAL. Being frugal, they say, is "the cornerstone of wealth-building."[4]

> **Being frugal is "the cornerstone of wealth-building."**

Long before Stanley and Danko started talking to millionaires, another man of remarkable financial means offered a similar piece of advice: "Do not wear yourself out to get rich," Solomon says in Proverbs 23:4, "have the wisdom to show restraint." Teaching your children the value of restraint and discipline over consumption and immediate gratification is one of the best financial gifts you could ever provide. In fact, Ecclesiastes 7:11–12 finds this type of legacy far more valuable than any monetary blessing:

> Wisdom, like an inheritance, is a good thing
>   and benefits those who see the sun.
> Wisdom is a shelter as money is a shelter,
> but the advantage of knowledge is this:
>   that wisdom preserves the life of its possessor.

. . . AND TO THEIR CHILDREN

Declining a parent's offer of financial aid can be one of the most difficult decisions an adult child may ever have to make. Not only do you risk alienating your folks, but you have to wrestle with the often overwhelming temptation to fall back into the comfortable, secure world of your upbringing.

When Trey and Anna turned down Trey's parents' offer of a down payment on a home in a pricey neighborhood, they knew, intuitively, what Stanley and Danko learned from their research: that living in such neighborhoods requires more than just an ability to pay the mortgage. Nicer clothing, attractive landscaping, home maintenance, finer automobiles, more expensive furnishings, and higher property taxes all come with the package and add up to one big bill—meaning that the original down payment gift would put them on a treadmill of consumption (and, most probably, continued dependence on Trey's parents).

Trey welcomed his God-given responsibility to provide for his family. He understood what it meant to "leave" his parents. Just as important, though, was Trey and Anna's willingness to "cleave" to one another. The biblical use of this term implies the need to "cling to" or "pursue" your spouse. The fact that Trey was wise enough to resist the economic assistance bodes well for his financial future. The fact that he and Anna presented a strong, united front in the face of financial temptation bodes even better for the future of their marriage.

One of the issues Trey and Anna faced was their common desire to see Anna stop working when they started a family. Not every two-income couple shares this goal. In the coming chapter, we'll look at the modern phenomenon of the working mother. Is a second income worth the trade-offs? Should you (or your wife) work outside your home? Whatever your perspective is, remember the lesson from this chapter: Cleaving to your spouse—pursuing unity in the face of difficult decisions—is just as important (if not more so) than leaving Mom and Dad's wallet behind.

Chapter Nine

Wives in the Workforce

An Objective Look at the Two-Income Family

The screen door slammed, and a moment later, Gail heard the sound her husband's keys always made as he tossed them onto the counter. She hurried to the kitchen and was just in time to see him dip a spoon into the Brunswick stew that simmered on the stove. "Mm-mmm," Alan said appreciatively, "I could smell this from the end of the driveway!"

"Well, we're all set to eat. Will you pour the drinks? I'll call the girls."

Becca and Ashley raced each other to the table, their giggles reverberating off the dining room walls. Becca's smile faded when she looked at her plate. "Ugh. Lima beans. Does Brunswick stew have to have lima beans?"

"It does if the cook is from Baltimore!" her father teased, ruffling his five-year-old's hair.

"And speaking of which, how did the interview go?"

Gail had spent the better part of her morning in an office near Baltimore's Inner Harbor, talking with a sales manager at a small pharmaceutical company. "Well, they offered me the job."

"That's terrific! But I'm surprised you found out so quickly."

"So am I. I was a little worried that being out of the job market for so long might hurt my chances, but they didn't seem to care. I think the fact that I'm a nurse was a big plus—they said they wanted someone who would be comfortable working with the medical staff and talking to the doctors about how the drugs work and all."

"When do you start?" Alan asked.

"In two weeks. I—"

"Start what, Mommy?" Ashley, their eight-year-old, wanted to know.

"Mommy got a job, darling."

"Why?"

"Well . . ." Gail looked at her husband. "Daddy and I thought that if I could earn some money, we could get a bigger house someday soon. Wouldn't you girls like to have your own rooms?"

Becca and Ashley looked at each other. "Maybe," Ashley said, speaking for both of them. "But who will take care of us? Amy's mom works and she has a mean baby-sitter!"

"Oh, I'll be home when you get home from school," Gail laughed. "It's a sales job—I can set my own hours. And besides, I sometimes get lonely at home without you. I used to have a job before you girls were born, you know."

"You did? Like Daddy?" Becca looked from one parent to the other.

"Well, sort of," Alan said. "I work in an office. Your mother worked in a hospital."

"Was it fun? Did you get to give people shots?" asked Ashley.

"Yes, and yes," Gail laughed again. "Now eat your supper. When I go back to work, you might not be getting things like Brunswick stew so much—it takes too long to make."

Ashley winked at Becca. "You know what that means?" she whispered.

"Yeah!" Becca almost shouted. "No more lima beans!"

Today, according to numbers obtained from the Bureau of Labor Statistics, two-income families outnumber single-income families more than three to one. In families with children under age eighteen, almost half of all mothers work full-time, while approximately one-fifth work part-time, and almost one-third are not in the labor force at all.

Bill Mattox, a consultant for the Family Research Council and other organizations, reads the statistics this way: Mothers, he says, fall into three general—and approximately equal—categories: One-third are nonemployed, choosing to stay home with their children; one-third are career-oriented, working full-time, year-round; and one-third are part-timers or temporarily employed full-time, organizing their jobs and work schedules around their families' needs. This last group, the part-time/temporaries, includes women who work fewer hours, shorter weeks, or for just part of the year (such as during the school year or for the Christmas season).

Looking at these numbers, it's not difficult to see why women—specifically, women with children at home—face a tough choice when deciding whether to work or stay home. A significant percentage of women have aligned themselves with each position. Is there any way to tell which group has made the right choice?

> *We do not believe it is an unqualified "sin" for a mother to work, even when the job takes her away from home. At the same time, though, we do not think that working is a woman's "right," regardless of her family situation.*

Are mothers who choose to pursue a career and work outside the home making a mistake? Are they sacrificing their families for a paycheck and the things that money can buy? Or, are their stay-at-home counterparts the ones who are missing out, unable to enjoy the tangible rewards of money, peer esteem, and the chance to use their marketplace skills and sharpen their intellects? What about the part-timers? Do they have the best of both worlds?

We can't answer these questions. Contrary to the philosophy embraced by many Christians today, we do not believe it is an unqualified "sin" for a mother to work, even when the job takes her away from home. At the same time, though, we do not think that working is a woman's "right," regardless of her family situation. Every couple must prayerfully choose for themselves the path that they should take.

Rather than counsel you on how to land a job, leave the workforce, or juggle the demands of a family and a career, we want to use this chapter to give you the information you need to make a wise, informed, and prayerful decision about your place in—or out of—the workforce. We can't tell you which path to take, but we can help you examine the trade-offs, costs, and sacrifices that will inevitably mark your decision, no matter which choice you make.

A note of qualification belongs here. Since this is a book about money and communication within the context of a marriage, the generalizations and information included in this chapter may not apply to single mothers. Raising a family without a husband's income (and, in some cases, without any form of child support), single mothers face their own set of unique challenges, restrictions, and economic trade-offs. Furthermore, our comments are, for the most part, aimed at couples who have children. In general, the decision of whether or not a wife should work is much more complicated when the wife is also a mother; if she does not have children, there is typically less of a need for her to stay home. In this chapter, then, we will use the terms "woman," "wife," and "mother" interchangeably.

WHY WOMEN WORK

Let's begin by looking at three of the most common reasons why women—wives and mothers—work: Women work because of societal norms and pressures, because of the desire for a creative outlet, and because of a need (whether real or perceived) for additional income.

Women Work Because Society Tells Them To

Popular culture has lumped mothers into two categories: those who work outside the home, and those who are "just a mom." Somewhere along the way, we have bought into the idea that staying home to raise a family is a second-rate job, one in which women "waste their education" or fail to "pull their own weight" by making a financial contribution to the family. For a stay-home mother who does not get a paycheck, who lacks adult companionship, and who gets little or no recognition for her job, accusations like these can be devastating to her sense of self-worth or purpose.

Husbands, if you and your wife agree that she should not work outside the home, you need to provide her with three things: (1) verbal praise and affirmation for the job she does as a wife and mother, (2) tangible at-home support to help her cope with the physical and emotional demands of mothering, and (3) a long-term perspective to keep both of you focused on the reasons behind your decision and the goals you have for your family.

Judy has led women's Bible studies for many years, and several of her groups have been made up of young mothers. As we worked on this chapter, we were reminded of a true story she told one of these groups years ago. A man arrived home from work to find his wife close to tears, exhausted from a long day at home with their two preschool-aged boys. "I feel like all I did today was break up fights and enforce discipline," the tired wife said. "Climbing on the furniture, calling each other names, throwing food—you name it, they did it. I must have spanked Tommy and Jimmy three or four times each!"

> *Sometimes a woman's fear of losing her marketability stems from a real, justifiable threat. In other cases, the threat is more imaginary than genuine.*

The husband considered the situation and then took his wife into his arms. "Do you mean to tell me," he said, "that you have spent the entire day *building character* into our sons?"

As any mother will tell you, this kind of long-term thinking—looking down the road to see future rewards for current efforts—can provide valuable motivation in a relatively thankless job.

Closely related to the woman who works because society tells her to is the mother who keeps her job or reenters the workforce in order to maintain her competitive edge. While we were writing this chapter, we heard about a mother who returned to the workplace after a six-year absence because, as she put it, "I am about to turn forty, and if I wait any longer no one will want to hire me. Companies would rather have someone younger, whose skills are fresh and who has a longer work life ahead of them."

Sometimes a woman's fear of losing her marketability stems from a real, justifiable threat. In other cases, the threat is more imaginary than genuine. Either way, though, you don't want to make a fear-based decision. If losing market skills or a competitive edge is a concern for you, step back and evaluate your situation. Ask yourself several questions: Are there courses I can take or certifications I should pursue to keep my skills or degrees current? Are there career paths other than the one I am trained for which interest me? What's the worst that could happen if I do not return to the workplace right now? Most importantly, why do I *really* want to work? Is my decision based on a genuine need or desire for employment—or am I catering to things like pride (in my position) or fear (that I will waste my education or training)? If you let factors such as pride and fear influence your thinking, you will never be able to make a wise, objective choice about whether to work, nor will you experience peace about your decision.

Women Work Because They Want a Creative Outlet

As we've told you, Judy did not work outside our home when our children were growing up. When Michael, our youngest, left home for college, Judy really struggled with the transition. She had spent thirty-one years taking care of five children—an effort that, I belatedly realized, took an incredible amount of creative and physical energy. When the kids were gone, Judy found herself wondering what she should do next. What was her purpose in life?

Had Judy worked while our children were growing up, the transition from mothering to empty-nesting would have been easier. As it was, she felt unprepared for a change that she knew would be difficult. But—as I have since discovered—my wife is not happy unless she drops into bed totally exhausted at night. All the energy she once channeled toward our children has found a new outlet. In addition to leading Bible studies and adapting to her new role as a grandmother, Judy recently stepped into a home-based business, selling a nutritional product we started using some time ago. Judy did not set out to get a job, but when she began to recommend and sell this particular product, she discovered that it was a wonderful outlet for her talents and abilities. After more than three decades of focusing on our children and our home, she welcomed a fresh direction for her creative energy.

As God's children, we are commanded to work, to "do something useful with our hands" (see Ephesians 4:28). For many women, caring for a family taps just a part of their usefulness. Some mothers take great delight in exercising their God-given talents by volunteering at schools or in community organizations, leading or participating in Bible studies, or pursuing various hobbies and interests. Sometimes, these pursuits come with a paycheck attached. The woman in Proverbs 31, for example, cooks, sews, and gardens to provide for her family. She also trades and sells in the marketplace, burning the midnight oil to ensure that her work is profitable. She watches over her household, cares for the poor, and makes money in the marketplace—three creative and useful pursuits that win her praise from her children, her husband, and the community leaders perched at the gates to her city.

If the image of the Proverbs 31 woman leaves you feeling exhausted or depressed by the thought of trying to measure up to her unqualified success, take heart: Many Bible scholars believe that she is not a real woman, but a composite of many noble and virtuous qualities. Even so, her endeavors at home and in the marketplace open the door for contemporary women to prayerfully consider where they should direct their energies and talents. For some, it will be as a full-time, stay-home mother. For others, creative energy may find an outlet in the workplace.

As you make your decision, take another look at the purpose statement you drafted in chapter one. Will you be more apt to meet your goals by focusing your creative energy at home or in an outside job? If you are looking for a way to use your talents and abilities, is there a home-based business or ministry opportunity you should consider? Would your family—and your purpose statement—be better served if you postponed a career move for a year or two, or perhaps much longer? If you opt to work outside your home, can you use some of the money you earn to hire domestic help to free up more of your nonworking hours? Don't limit yourself to the one-dimensional question of whether or not you should work; instead, open your eyes to all of the alternatives.

Women Work to Make Money

In families where the wife's job provides a second income, the most common reason she works is not societal pressure or the need for a creative outlet, but to make money. Often, this need for additional income is driven by material desires and an expanded or inflated lifestyle. In some cases, though, our current financial system—

including higher tax rates, inflated prices for homes and cars, company layoffs, and skyrocketing college costs—makes it almost impossible to survive on just one income.

Wives, if you think you *need* to work—that is, if your family requires your salary for its very survival—you might be right. Then again, you might be wrong. Have you ever stopped to consider just how much of a financial contribution you are actually making to your family's lifestyle?

> *To make an informed, objective decision about the relative worth of a wife's paycheck, you need to accurately evaluate the size and impact of the second income as it pertains to the family budget.*

My colleague and fellow financial author Larry Burkett says, "The sad truth is that most working mothers sacrifice time with their families with little or nothing to show for it. Most of the average working mother's wages are consumed by taxes, transportation, child care costs, and clothing. Even when a working mother's income is large enough to substantially add to the family's budget, the surplus is often consumed by an expanded lifestyle."[1]

To make an informed, objective decision about the relative worth of a wife's paycheck, you need to accurately evaluate the size and impact of the second income as it pertains to the family budget. If you have not already done so, take a few moments to assess your situation:

1. Write down your gross (pre-tax) income.

2. Deduct the amount you normally tithe.

3. Deduct the amount you pay in federal, state, and social security taxes. (Typically, taxes eat up anywhere from 35 to 45 percent of your income, with self-employed people at the higher end of the scale. If you are unsure how much to figure in this exercise, check last year's tax return or assume an average rate of about 40 percent.)

4. The amount you have left over is your net income. Now deduct the cost of all your work-related expenses. Remember to list things like transportation costs, day care expenses (less whatever tax credit you receive, if any), and other items such as career clothing,

domestic help, and restaurant lunches or take-out meals—those things that you would not spend money on if you did not work.

5. The total, after you account for taxes, tithe, and expenses, is your contribution to your family's income. Is it worth it? Here is what your personal economic analysis might look like:

WHAT IS YOUR PAYCHECK REALLY WORTH?			
Wife's Salary	$15,000	$30,000	$45,000	You*
1. Giving	1,500	3,000	4,500	
2. Federal Tax	4,200	8,400	12,600	
3. State Tax	750	1,500	2,250	
4. FICA Tax	1,148	2,295	3,443	
5. Child Care	9,600	9,600	9,600	
6. Transportation	1,200	1,200	1,200	
7. Meals	1,000	1,000	1,000	
8. Extra Clothes/ Dry Cleaning	600	600	600	
9. Miscellaneous	600	600	600	
Wife's Expenses	$20,598	$28,195	$35,793	
Salary Minus Expenses	($5,598)	$1,805	$9,208	
10. Plus Child Care Credit	2,592	1,920	1,920	
Net Additional Family Income	($3,006)	$3,725	$11,128	

*Use the last column to figure out what a second income is really worth in your family, based on the following guidelines:

1. Giving: 10% of income.
2. Federal Tax: 28% tax rate.
3. State Tax: 5% tax rate.
4. FICA Tax: 7.65% tax rate (15.3% if self-employed).
5. Child Care: Two children at an average cost of $400 per child per month.
6. Transportation: $100 a month (additional gas, maintenance, and repairs).
7. Meals: $20 a week for 50 weeks.
8. Extra Clothes/Drycleaning: $50 per month.
9. Miscellaneous: $50 per month (personal grooming, convenience foods, etc.).
10. Plus Child Care Credit: Between 20–30% of child care expenses depending on income.

WEIGHING THE TRADE-OFFS

Regardless of whether you choose to work or stay home, there will be trade-offs and sacrifices to consider. Working mothers may find themselves missing a toddler's first step, a second-grader's school performance, or a teenager's soccer tournament. They may wrestle with frustration as they return home at night to prepare dinner and cram

> *Regardless of whether you choose to work or stay home, there will be trade-offs and sacrifices to consider.*

a day's worth of household chores and family communication into a few precious hours. In juggling the polarized demands of their jobs and families, they may—as one mother we talked to put it—experience "stress times ten."

On the other hand, stay-home moms may feel isolated in a world dominated mainly by children, or bored with a household routine that varies little from day to day. Confronted with other full-time mothers who seem to thrive on everything from dirty diapers to PTA meetings, some stay-homers may struggle with their own sense of inadequacy. And the financial sacrifices associated with one-income living—from dining out less to giving up things like household help, family vacations, or private schools—can lead to discouragement and doubt.

When her sons were young, Elizabeth worked part-time as a legal secretary while her mother cared for the children two or three days per week. Elizabeth enjoyed her career and assumed that, as her children grew and went off to school, she would be able to return to work full-time. But when her younger son, Thomas, was diagnosed with a mild learning disability, everything changed. In addition to driving him to and from classes at a special school located forty minutes from their home, Elizabeth wanted to be available to help Thomas with his schoolwork in the afternoons. She realized that she simply could not work full-time and meet her son's special needs; in fact, she and her husband decided that the best option, at least for the time being, would be for her to stop working entirely.

Although Elizabeth felt she had made the right choice, she was not prepared for the sense of loneliness and isolation that engulfed her when she quit her job. She did not have any close friends who were full-time mothers, and as she drove the long trip to and from Thomas's school, she brooded over her current lack of intellectual stimulation and adult companionship. She missed the office camaraderie—not to mention her paycheck. How, she wondered, did other stay-home moms do it?

DEVELOPING YOUR EXIT STRATEGY

Like the vast majority of women who make the transition from office to home, Elizabeth failed to consider the potential consequences of her decision and plan for the changes she would encounter. Our firm counsels clients on financial issues such as retirement or transferring ownership in a family business, and we often work with people to develop an effective "exit strategy." In essence, an exit strategy is a "how-to" plan for leaving the workplace (or your own business) so that the transition is as smooth, deliberate, and successful as possible. Without such a plan, many retirees or former business owners find themselves floundering amid doubt and a lack of clear direction about the future.

In his book *Women Leaving the Workplace*, Larry Burkett points to a growing migration of women from the workplace to the home. Of the more than six hundred women Burkett surveyed about their decision to stop working, 92 percent said they wished they had planned better for the move from the office to the home. And, of the mothers who later went *back* to work, nearly 100 percent said their return to the workplace was due to "lack of planning" before they quit.[2]

As we mentioned earlier, our aim in this book is not to tell you how to find or leave a job, but rather to help you consider the factors involved in your decision. If, however, you and your spouse are committed to living on the husband's salary alone, Burkett's "how-to" book can help you make the transition from two incomes to one. In addition to offering tips from stay-home moms and advice on budgeting time and money, the book provides information on issues such as taxes and insurance, and even includes a list of home-based businesses and other resources.

UNITY, UNITY, UNITY

As with every issue covered in this book, Judy and I cannot overstate the importance of unity between a husband and a wife. Whether a wife wants to pursue a career or devote herself to full-time mothering, she needs the full and unqualified support of her husband. Likewise, if a husband wants his wife to work (or if he asks her to stay home), he needs to know that she agrees with his thinking.

We know of one couple—Lucy and Bill—whose daughter was struggling in school, due primarily to a personality conflict with her teacher. As they considered the situation, Bill and Lucy felt that their best option was for Lucy to accept a teaching position in a local private school, where her employee tuition discount would make it financially possible for them to enroll their daughter. But as Lucy reflected on their decision, she grew increasingly concerned about the ramifications it would have on their lifestyle. "I knew that if I started teaching," she said, "it would throw off the whole balance of our family life. Financially, we could afford to send our daughter to private school—but the noneconomic cost would be too much to bear."

An implicit assumption in decision making is that the choice you ultimately make will satisfy various personal objectives and priorities. For Lucy, the ability to maintain balance in her family life was a high priority—one she was not willing to sacrifice. Fortunately, she and Bill were wise enough to realize that Lucy's teaching job (and the private school option it afforded) was not their only alternative. They continued to pray about the situation, and ultimately, the problem was resolved when school administrators offered to transfer their daughter to another class.

When you have to make an important decision, one of the best ways to objectively review and weigh your alternatives is to map them out in a decision matrix. Judy and I have used a decision matrix to help us make all sorts of decisions with our family, from choosing vacation or college destinations to deciding which house to buy or what career path to pursue. Not only can a decision matrix help foster unity by providing a way to quantify and measure alternatives, but it will also allow you to avoid making decisions based on your "feelings." Good decisions fulfill objectives, not emotions.

A decision matrix is based on a six-step process:

1.   *Write out or verbalize the actual decision you need to make.*

For a wife who is considering a career or part-time job, the decision might be worded this way: "I must choose the best way to spend my time, my talents, and my energy."

2.   *List all your objectives that relate to this decision, both quantitative and qualitative.*

Think about the things you want to maximize and minimize. For example, in deciding whether or not a wife should work, the objectives might include:

Maximize time with husband and children

Maximize use of skills and talents

Maximize income

Maximize character development in children

Maximize time for kids' friends, school functions, activities, etc.

Minimize boredom

Minimize commute time

Minimize costs (child care, transportation, etc.)

Minimize stress

3.   *Rank your objectives in order of their importance.*

Since you can't have everything, there will always be some degree of conflict in your priorities. Give each objective a number valued from one to five, with "5" being a "non-negotiable" priority and "1" being an objective you could live without.

Obviously, the objectives and their relative rankings will be different for each individual, since any given goal or priority will matter more to one person than it does to someone else. For instance, Callie is a writer who has a husband and three young children. To her, being available to spend time with them matters more, relatively speaking, than earning additional income. When Callie ranked her objectives, her priorities looked like this:

Rank	Objective
5	Maximize time with husband and children
5	Maximize use of skills and talents
2	Maximize income
5	Maximize character development in children
4	Maximize time for kids' friends, functions, etc.
1	Minimize boredom
1	Minimize commute time
3	Minimize costs (child care, transportation, etc.)
4	Minimize stress

4.   List all possible alternatives.

Write down all of your options, no matter how unappealing or unattractive they may initially appear. As author and management consultant Peter Drucker says, "A decision is a judgment ... a choice among alternatives. Rarely is the choice between right or wrong, but rather the best choice between almost right and probably wrong." And since your decision can never be better than your best known alternative, the more alternatives you can come up with, the better your chances will be of settling on the choice that is "almost right."

In Callie's case, her alternatives included staying home with her children, working in a full-time career (as she had before her children were born), and working part-time outside her home. You might have additional options or possibilities to consider.

5.   Evaluate each alternative based on how it fulfills your objectives and priorities.

If an alternative meets a particular objective, give it "points" based on the numerical ranking you assigned to that objective in step three. If the alternative allows you to fully maximize (or minimize) an objective, give it the full value of its rank. If it contributes toward the objective but does not entirely fulfill it, assign it a partial score. The idea is to get yourself thinking in terms of *objectives*, rather than *alternatives*.

When Callie evaluated her alternatives, her matrix looked like this:

CALLIE'S DECISION MATRIX				
		Stay Home/ Not in the Workforce	Part-time Job	Full-time Career
Rank	**Objective**			
5	Maximize time with husband and children	5	2	0
5	Maximize use of skills and talents	0	3	5
2	Maximize income	0	1	2
5	Maximize character development in children	5	2	0
4	Maximize time for kids' friends, functions, etc.	4	2	0
1	Minimize boredom	1	1	1
1	Minimize commute time	1	0	0
3	Minimize costs (child care, transportation, etc.)	3	0	0
4	Minimize stress	0	0	0
	Total Points	23	11	8

6. *Choose the alternative that best meets your objectives and priorities.*

Add up the "points" under each alternative based on the evaluation you did in step five. In Callie's case, staying at home received the highest score (23). Even so, Callie was not entirely comfortable with that alternative. She welcomed the additional income that would come with working, but even more than that, the "stay home" alternative ran counter to her deep conviction that God wanted her to use her professional skills and talents for some specific jobs and projects, both paid and unpaid. Given the importance of the "skills and talents" objective, Callie began to wonder if there might be another option she had not originally considered.

Two weeks later, Callie got her answer. A home security company for which she had once designed a brochure called to see if she would write a few articles for their quarterly newsletter on a free-lance basis. As she considered the company's offer, a new idea began to take shape in Callie's mind: If there was a market for freelance writing (and she felt sure that there was), she might be able to network with her former business contacts and develop a writing career from her home! Intrigued by the prospect, Callie put the "freelancing" alternative into her decision matrix. Then, the results looked like this:

CALLIE'S DECISION MATRIX

Rank	Objective	Stay Home/ Not in the Workforce	Part-time Job	Full-time Career	Freelance/ home-based business
5	Maximize time with husband and children	5	2	0	4
5	Maximize use of skills and talents	0	3	5	5
2	Maximize income	0	1	2	1
5	Maximize character development in children	5	2	0	4
4	Maximize time for kids' friends, functions, etc.	4	2	0	3
1	Minimize boredom	1	1	1	1
1	Minimize commute time	1	0	0	1
3	Minimize costs (child care, transportation, etc.)	3	0	0	3
4	Minimize stress	0	0	0	0
	Total Points	23	11	8	22

Again, staying at home fulfilled more of Callie's objectives—but only by the slimmest margin over the freelancing option. And the difference between freelancing and working in a full- or part-time position left Callie wondering why she hadn't thought of freelancing right from the start! But that is exactly the point: sometimes the best alternative does not present itself until you have already considered—and discarded—the obvious. If you lack an alternative that meets or fulfills most of your objectives, don't get discouraged. Ask God to open your eyes and your mind to alternatives you might not have considered before, and then weigh these new possibilities in light of your objectives. In our experience, the "either/or" options we tend to consider at the outset of any decision usually transform themselves into another solution that is often more creative—and almost always more appealing—than anything we had thought of at first.

Once you have worked your way through the decision matrix, evaluate the risk associated with your decision. Ask yourself two questions: (1) What's the worst thing that could happen if I pursued this alternative? and (2) How likely is that "worst case scenario" to occur? The answer to these questions will help you assess the level of risk associated with your top choice. If the risk factor is too high, eliminate that alternative and focus on the option with the next highest score.

Put another way, *are you comfortable with the decision?* If Callie had chosen the alternative with the highest score (23), she would have stayed home and not worked at all. But by moving on to her second alternative, freelancing, she discovered that it was actually a better choice, in terms of the objectives it fulfilled. Again, when you begin to see a decision in terms of the objectives or priorities that it fulfills (rather than looking at the alternatives themselves), the best option often becomes obvious.

Judy and I had a similar experience when we applied this decision-making technique to my career path nearly thirty years ago. Then, staying in Indianapolis (where we grew up) received the highest total point score. We did not, however, want to raise our family there; the "risk factor" associated with the fast-paced, materialistic lifestyle we had settled into in that city was too great. Therefore, despite its high ranking, we eliminated that option from the matrix and pursued the second-highest score instead, which ultimately took us to Atlanta.

As you complete the decision matrix, the rankings you assign to each of your objectives should line up with the priorities reflected in your marriage purpose statement, developed in chapter one. Would the additional income or creative outlet provided by a wife's job enhance your overall objectives, or would it take your focus off of your ultimate goals? Would a part-time or home-based business contribute to the fulfillment of your purpose in marriage, or would it open the door to stress or confusion in your home? How would a commitment to full-time mothering affect your lives—and your children's lives—five, ten, or twenty years down the road?

Only you can answer questions like these. Our goal as the authors of this book is not to tell you what to do with your money, your talents, or your life. Rather, our aim is to give you the principles and tools you need to make wise decisions. If all you take away from this book is a deliberate, prayerfully developed, written purpose statement for your marriage, that alone will be well worth your time and effort.

We have already seen how a well-crafted mission statement can help you establish budget parameters, evaluate career moves, and make important financial and practical decisions for your family. In the coming chapter, we will look at the issue of charitable giving, which—more than almost any other subject—can reflect the true measure of your unity and ability to communicate effectively about your finances.

Chapter Ten

Check(book) Please!

Finding Common Ground for Giving

"The Young Marrieds class at church doesn't have a teacher this year," Don said, looking at his wife, Tracy. "The Sunday school coordinator called me today to see if we'd be interested in teaching the class. What do you think?"

"Oh, Don," Tracy sighed, "You know I'd like to help. But isn't that the class where someone always seems to need money? If we teach it and one of those couples gets in trouble, we'll be the first ones they come to for help."

"So? Is that such a bad thing?"

"It is if we don't have the money."

"Well," Don smiled, "Let's cross that bridge when we come to it. I'll call the church and let them know we'll do it."

Two weeks after she and Don started teaching, Tracy's fears were realized. A young couple, married less than a year, confided to the class that they did not have enough money to pay the rent on their small apartment, and they worried that they would find themselves without a place to live.

"Tracy," Don whispered, as the group began to pray for the couple, "we have to help them. We have the money to give."

"How do you know?" Tracy whispered back. "I pay the bills, and I can tell you right now that we do not have the money to give!"

"Well, I'm sure we can find it. We'll just cut back someplace this month. And don't forget, I'll be getting a commission check in the next week or two."

Tracy bent her head, trying to pray and think at the same time. Don had a gift and a heart for giving—that much was clear. From the very beginning of their marriage he had pushed for a higher level of giving than Tracy felt comfortable with. Don would give someone the shirt off his back, while Tracy—who worked part-time as a financial planner—kept a close eye on their family budget.

Despite her misgivings, Tracy realized that, above everything, she wanted to honor her husband. She knew she would feel guilty if she tried to crush his generous spirit. "Okay, God," she silently prayed, "you say that everything belongs to you. We'll give this money . . . let's see how you will replace it."

Don and Tracy's story is all too familiar. The only difference is that, with the people Judy and I talk to, it's often the wife who wants to give and the husband who holds her back. If the wife is a Christian and her husband is not, she may wonder whether she ought to tithe in obedience to the Lord—even if it means offending, angering, or dishonoring her husband.

> *If the wife is a Christian and her husband is not, she may wonder whether she ought to tithe in obedience to the Lord—even if it means offending, angering, or dishonoring her husband.*

Other common questions center around *how much* to give. One couple we talked with became frustrated when, as newlyweds, they realized they had very different perceptions about what constituted an appropriate tithe. And even when husbands and wives agree on what percentage of their income they want to give, they don't always share the same vision when it comes to deciding *where* the money should go.

Finding common ground for giving is one of the most interesting communication challenges couples face today. In this chapter, we want to give you several principles you can use to address issues like how much to give, where to give, and how to make giving a vibrant and enriching element of your marriage. As one woman told us, once she and her husband understood the principles of giving and learned to see it as part of their overall financial plan, generosity became more than just a "Christian duty." It became a fun, rewarding, and life-changing experience.

TO GIVE OR NOT TO GIVE

What happens when you want to give and your spouse doesn't?

When Judy and I were first married, neither of us were Christians and tithing had no place in our family budget. Later, after Judy became a Christian, she began to read in Scripture about the commandments and promises that were tied to giving. She knew, though, that to talk about these things would have turned me off, spiritually. I wasn't interested in anything that would decrease my net worth—and when you give money away, you always have less of it left for yourself.

God doesn't need your money, but he does want your relationship to work.

So Judy didn't talk about giving, or read me any Bible verses about generosity, tithing, or giving in obedience to God's commands. In retrospect, I think she made a wise decision. She recognized—whether consciously or not—the first principle of finding common ground for giving: *God doesn't need your money, but he does want your relationship to work.*

God doesn't need your money. As Psalm 50:10 puts it, the Lord owns "the cattle on a thousand hills." Your financial contribution—no matter how large it is—isn't going to make a difference to God's bottom line.

God does, however, want your relationship to work. He wants his children to put their trust in him, and as you may remember from chapter one, he designed marriage as a means for procreation, promoting his kingdom, and providing for our needs. To fulfill these purposes effectively, you have got to have a good marriage. In other words, the question you should ask yourself is not "Should I give, even if it means dishonoring or alienating my spouse?" but "What actions (or attitudes) on my part would be most apt to (1) bring my spouse to the place where he or she will trust Christ? and (2) strengthen our marriage relationship?"

HOW MUCH SHOULD WE GIVE?

People have often asked us how much they should give, percentage-wise, or whether they should figure the amount based on their gross or net income. Unfortunately for the folks who want a simple answer, the Bible does not offer any set formula for calculating an appropriate tithe. The *tithe* (which means "tenth") mentioned in Malachi 3:10 is just one of several giving levels; elsewhere in the Old Testament, God asks his people to give as much as twenty-three percent of their income to be used in the temple and for various mercy ministries (see Leviticus 27:30; Numbers 18:21; Deuteronomy 14:22).

In the New Testament, the guidelines are much less specific, percentage-wise. God asks that we give willingly, cheerfully, and in accordance with how we have been prospered—that is, we are to give in proportion to the amount we have received (see 2 Corinthians 8:12; 9:7). Scripture also advocates generosity, pointing out that "Whoever sows sparingly will also reap sparingly, and whoever sows generously will also reap generously" (2 Corinthians 9:6). In other words, instead of asking "How much is enough to give?" a better question might be "How generous—and how blessed—do I want to be?"

Because there are no "right" answers to the "How much?" question, the second principle in finding common ground for giving is this: *Deciding how much to give requires prayer, perspective, and—at times—a willingness to wait.*

If you aren't sure how much to give—or, more specifically, how much God wants you to give—start by *praying* about the matter. Tracy and Don, the couple whose story you read at the beginning of this chapter, had differing views about how much they should give: Don wanted to give a minimum of fifteen percent of their income, while Tracy admitted to struggling with even a ten-percent tithe. When they committed to praying about the issue, the tension in their relationship disappeared. Don realized that Tracy was sincere in her desire to honor him, while she took comfort in the fact that he would not leave her financially "abandoned" in his zeal for generous living.

To get the right *perspective* on giving, find out what the Bible says about how much you should give. In my book *Generous Living*, we identify three biblically based levels at which Christians can give: The "Should Give" level (a basic percentage, prayerfully calculated as a proportion of your income), the "Could Give" level (the amount you would be able to give if you were willing to sacrifice something), and the "Would Give" level (the amount you would pre-commit or earmark for giving, should an unexpected surplus show up in your budget). Tracy and Don agreed to start giving at the "Should Give" level, and then made a commitment to exploring ways they could move to the next level—sacrificial giving—in the future.

The third element in deciding how much to give—the willingness to *wait*—is an important safeguard for your relationship. Once Tracy and Don settled on a minimum giving level, they agreed to wait before they increased their giving—a decision which allowed them time to pray about and plan for the increase. Moses commanded the Israelites to do the same thing in Numbers 9. When some of the Israelites wanted to rush their offering to the Lord in order to become ceremonially clean before they celebrated the Passover, Moses told them to hold off. "Wait," he said, "until I find out what the LORD commands concerning you" (verse 8).

> *Unlike a delay that stems from laziness or procrastination, there is nothing wrong with a purposeful wait.*

Unlike a delay that stems from laziness or procrastination, there is nothing wrong with a purposeful wait. Remember, your relationship—and the unity you enjoy before the Lord—is more important to God than your money.

WHERE SHOULD WE GIVE?

Judy and I know a woman named Anne who wants to give money almost every time she hears about a financial need—regardless of how much she knows about a particular organization, the people involved, or the ministry's track record. Her husband, Sam, is much less inclined to give, particularly when he does not have a personal interest in the organization.

It seemed to Anne that whenever she wanted to respond to an appeal, Sam would hold her back. Eventually, she began to see him as insensitive, stingy, and hard-hearted. But when she confronted him with her feelings, Sam defended himself. "I don't want to give based on an emotional urge," he said. "I want our giving to be responsible and purposeful. I'm not opposed to giving to any particular ministry—I just want to think about it first."

Hugh Maclellan would appreciate Sam's perspective. Hugh serves on our firm's Board of Directors and heads up one of the country's largest Christian charitable foundations. "Most people," he says, "give in response to emotional or persistent appeals. Very few of us take the time to check out an organization to see whether the need is justified or whether the group can produce results." Consequently, Hugh estimates that fully half of all giving is ineffective.

Judy and I have used seven critical questions to help us pinpoint opportunities for effective and strategic giving. These questions, which are covered in greater detail in *Generous Living*, are adapted from material developed by our friend Pat MacMillan, who is a management consultant and the author of *Hiring Excellence*. As you evaluate an organization's effectiveness, ask:

1. Are the leaders marked by godly characteristics, including character, integrity, and vision? Are they competent in their jobs?
2. Is the ministry active in places where God is obviously at work?
3. Is the ministry or organization innovative? Are they willing to experiment, challenge the routine, and take advantage of unusual or uncommon opportunities?
4. Is the ministry growing and cooperative? Are they getting results, and will they work with other Christian groups or organizations?
5. Is the ministry goal-oriented? Do they have a clear sense of what God wants them to do, and how he wants them to do it?
6. Is the ministry accountable? Do they measure progress and results, or are they content with mere "activity"? Who do the leaders report to?
7. Is the ministry endorsed by a strong track record? What kind of "fruits" have their efforts produced in the past?

In addition to answering these questions, Judy and I recognize that people give where they have relationships. For example, if your teenager is active in a youth group or high school ministry, you may sense God calling you to contribute to that organization. If your church launches an evangelistic mission in the Dominican Republic, you may be inclined to give money—or even your vacation time— to support the effort. As you consider the limitless possibilities for giving, think about where God has placed you, and why.

For couples who want to find common ground for giving, the third principle is this: *To maximize your effectiveness, you need to have a common vision.* Do you have a heart for evangelism? Is discipling new Christians—teaching, equipping, and training them—exciting to you? Are you compassionate toward the needy or eager to meet the physical needs of the poor? Do you have other concerns for your neighborhood, your community, or the world?

When Anne and Sam discussed their individual visions for giving, they realized that they shared many interests and objectives. Using the following worksheet, they were able to prayerfully map out a list of people and organizations they wanted to support, noting which ministry objective each individual or organization was designed to fulfill. Working from their list, they reconciled Anne's emotional desire for generosity with Sam's need for a thoughtful analysis of their priorities and the results that their giving could achieve.

GIVING AS PART OF THE PLAN

Once Sam and Anne developed a common vision for giving, they needed to think about the amount of money they wanted to give to each individual or organization listed on their giving worksheet. For Sam, who handled the family checkbook, this allocation phase was especially important, since he wanted to ensure that their budget would support their desired level of generosity.

To develop their plan for giving, Sam and Anne again listed the organizations and individuals they wanted to support. Beside each name, they penciled in an annual giving amount. Then they added the amounts to determine what total percentage of their budget they would need to designate for giving, if they wanted to reach their generosity goals.

Area of Influence	Organization/ Individual	Ministry Objective			
		Evangelism	Discipleship	The Needy	Other
Local	Church	✔	✔		
	Homeless Shelter	✔		✔	
	Museum				✔
National	Teen Outreach	✔	✔		
	Family Ministry		✔		
	Medical Research				✔
Global	Relief Organization	✔			
	Children's Fund			✔	
	Medical Outreach				✔

* Note: Sam wanted to give to medical research, since it provided help for human suffering, which he considered a kingdom principle. Likewise, Anne wanted to donate to a local museum, which she felt reflected the beauty of God's creation. While neither of these nonprofit organizations is a Christian ministry, we cannot fault Sam and Anne's decision. Giving—how much and to whom—should be the result of a prayerful conviction, rather than something that is done from legalistic motives. We do, however, want to offer one cautionary note: Just because something is tax deductible, it is not necessarily part of your tithe. Base your giving decisions chiefly on the need to please and honor God, rather than on a tax-wise strategy.

Sam and Anne understood the truth behind the fourth principle of finding common ground for giving: Planning to give is what makes generosity possible. It doesn't matter how much money you make. Without a preestablished plan for giving, you will never be able to give as much—or as willingly—as you otherwise would. Since needs almost always expand to meet income, you simply won't have anything left over to give, once your bills are paid. Likewise, when you begin your plan by asking "How much can we afford to give?" instead of "How much do we want to give?" you will never maximize your potential for generosity.

Base your giving decisions chiefly on the need to please and honor God, rather than on a tax-wise strategy.

For Judy and me, our giving plan is the best part of our budget. Each year, when we sit down to figure out where and how much we will give, we precommit a certain percentage of our income to our church and other ministries or organizations we want to support. Then we set aside an amount in a type of "slush fund," a discretionary category that we can draw on as we become aware of other financial needs. We have even invited our children to help us distribute some of this money, which reinforces their commitment to generous living and adds to the pleasure we take in giving. And because our giving is a predetermined part of our budget, generosity becomes a privilege and a joy, instead of a financial burden.

> *If you know where and when you are committed to giving, you can graciously refuse a request for money without feeling guilty or confused.*

Another benefit to having a plan for giving is that a plan can relieve the emotional pressure that often comes with financial appeals. If you know where and when you are committed to giving, you can graciously refuse a request for money without feeling guilty or confused. You will be free to give as Scripture commands in 2 Corinthians 9:7: "Each man should give what he has decided in his heart to give, not reluctantly or under compulsion, for God loves a cheerful giver."

Until you "decide in your heart" what and how you want to give—that is, until you make *a deliberate choice to give and establish a plan for implementing your decision*—you will never be able to give freely, cheerfully, and in a way that pleases the Lord.

RECOGNIZE THE REWARDS

Let's review the four principles involved in finding common ground for giving:

1. God doesn't need your money, but he wants your relationship to work.
2. Deciding how much to give requires prayer, perspective, and—at times—a willingness to wait.
3. To maximize your strategic giving, you need to have a common vision.
4. Planning to give is what makes generosity possible.

Remember Tracy and Don? When they put these principles into practice, it literally changed their marriage. Tracy had tears in her eyes as she told us about the transformation: Where opportunities to give had once created tension and division in their relationship, they became touchpoints for a common vision and a shared commitment to planned generosity. Thanks to their newfound unity, she and Don have agreed to make tithing a top financial priority, and they look forward to increasing their giving in the future. As Tracy says, "I used to think giving was a blessing to the receiver. Now I know it is designed to benefit us."

If you want to reap the rewards of a generous lifestyle, make giving part of your financial plan. You might have to start small, at first, especially if you and your spouse don't share a common vision for how generous you want to be or where you want your resources to be used. But if you commit to thinking, talking, and—most importantly—praying about giving, you will not be disappointed. Finding common ground for giving will improve your communication, enrich your relationship, and enhance your ultimate potential for making a difference in the kingdom of God. And when you plan properly, generosity can become one of the most satisfying and rewarding aspects of your marriage.

Chapter Eleven

Looking Ahead

Where Do We Go from Here?

At the outset of this book, we said that there is no such thing as a money problem. The successful resolution of every financial issue—from crafting a budget to coping with influential in-laws—almost always depends on one thing: Effective communication.

Think back to the principles outlined at the beginning of this book. *What is the purpose of money?* If you recall, money is chiefly a tool, a test, and a testimony. *What is the purpose of marriage?* Among other things, marriage is a means for procreation, promoting God's kingdom, and providing for your spouse. *What is the purpose of your marriage?* Specifically, what principles and priorities are reflected in the purpose statement you developed in chapter one?

Your answers to these questions will, to a large degree, determine your ability to tackle economic issues with a minimum of conflict or tension in your marriage. If you understand that money is a tool, for example, you will be open to exploring the ways it can be used. If you recognize that money is also a testimony, you will be better equipped to evaluate and prioritize your spending habits. And if you see marriage as more than just a vehicle for love and companionship, you will be able to move forward and take hold of the plan—the specific and wonderful purpose—that God has for you and your spouse.

Judy and I have been married for more than thirty-three years. During that time, we have dealt with all of the issues covered in this book, along with countless others. If there is one truth we have learned about solving problems, it is that *planning is a process*. Our habits and priorities are pretty well established at this point, yet we still depend on our planning weekends, date nights, and other communication tools to keep our marriage strong and our purpose statement in focus. In fact, now that we are "empty nesters," we can invest more time than ever in our relationship. Drawing on the habits formed in the past three decades, hardly a day goes by when we do not talk and interact with one another about the decisions, activities, and plans that lie ahead.

Planning is not a "once and for all" experience. The habits you form now will make communication easier in the years to come, but they will never remove or replace the perpetual need to invest time, work, and commitment into your marriage.

In the Old Testament, God gives Joshua the job of leading the Israelites into Canaan, the Promised Land. God's mission for Joshua is clear: "Be strong and courageous, because you will lead these people to inherit the land I swore to their forefathers to give them." Joshua knows that conquering the Promised Land will not be easy; in fact, he orders his men to show up "fully armed" for the battle ahead. But in addition to giving Joshua a purpose (claiming the land), God fortifies him with a promise: "Do not be terrified; do not be discouraged, for the LORD your God will be with you wherever you go" (Joshua 1:6, 9).

What is your purpose? Take another look at your mission statement. Is there a "land" that God is pointing you and your spouse toward, or a promise he wants you to claim? Whatever your prayerfully developed purpose or mission is, you can be sure of one thing: The Lord will be with you, wherever you go.

This promise is particularly comforting when you realize that the Israelites weren't the only ones who needed to gear up for a fight. All of us can expect to face battles from time to time—and, at some point in our marriages, we are apt to become discouraged or disillusioned. Discouragement can show up in many ways: debt can create bondage, investments can turn sour, and even pleasurable experiences like giving money to your children or your church can lead to tension and a lack of unity. Discouragement, in fact, can be Satan's greatest weapon. But God commands us *not* to be discouraged. Can we obey this commandment, even in the face of seemingly impossible odds? Yes! The key, again, is in the promise: "Do not be discouraged, for the LORD your God will be with you wherever you go."

When Joshua grew old, he summoned all the leaders and officials in Israel. Recognizing that his own death was imminent, he took the opportunity to reflect on everything God had accomplished in and through the Israelites: He built Abraham's family into a nation, he conquered Israel's enemies, and he gave them lush and prosperous cities to call their own. As Joshua recalled God's faithfulness, he challenged the Israelites to take a stand and choose whom they wanted to serve. Then, at the end of his speech, Joshua issued his own version of a purpose statement: "As for me and my household, we will serve the LORD" (Joshua 24:15).

Look down the road, toward the end of your life. Wouldn't it be great to look back and see a legacy of victories God had accomplished in and through your life?

Put yourself in Joshua's shoes. Look down the road, toward the end of your life. Wouldn't it be great to look back and see a legacy of victories God had accomplished in and through your life? Wouldn't it be satisfying to see your enemies—from financial concerns to marital conflict—lying conquered in your wake? Wouldn't it be wonderful to know that you—and your marriage—had fulfilled a God-given, powerful purpose?

This vision can become a reality. To strengthen your marriage and fulfill your purpose, start at the very beginning. Pray with your spouse. Ask God to show you his mission statement for your marriage. Ask him to point you toward the goals and objectives he wants you to pursue. Ask him to bring you and your spouse into unity as you work to understand and follow his directions.

Next, take time to plan. If you have not done so already, set a date right now for your first planning weekend. Again, it doesn't matter what your circumstances are: planning is everything. If you are properly prepared, you will be equipped to handle any financial question or concern that comes your way.

Finally, revisit your purpose statement. Having read this book, are there steps you need to take—such as dealing with debt, drafting a will, or making a plan for giving—to bring the day-to-day realities of your lives into line with your overall mission in life? Think of your purpose statement as a tool. Use it—and get comfortable with the way it feels in your hands as you continue to define your priorities and goals. Review it—and recognize that it can be reshaped as your family's needs and circumstances change. Revise it—and rely on it as the basis for all of the planning you do in the months and years ahead, remembering that when you follow God's directions, he will be with you wherever you go.

NOTES

CHAPTER ONE — Making a Statement

1. Howard Dayton, *Your Money Counts* (Longwood, Florida: Crown Ministries: 1996), 8.
2. Steven Covey, *The Seven Habits of Highly Effective People* (New York: Simon & Schuster, 1989), 108–109.

CHAPTER TWO — Can We Talk?

1. Barbara K. Mouser, *Five Aspects of a Woman* (Waxahachie, Texas: The International Council for Gender Studies, Inc., 1995), 2.44.
2. Ronald and Beverly Allen, *Liberated Traditionalism* (Sisters, Oregon: Multnomah Press, 1985), 124.
3. Larry Crabb, *The Silence of Adam* (Grand Rapids, Michigan: Zondervan, 1995), 11–12.

CHAPTER SEVEN — Where There's a Wife There's a Will

1. Zoe M. Hicks, *The Woman's Estate Planning Guide* (Chicago: NTC/Contemporary Publishing, 1998), 5.

CHAPTER EIGHT — Leaving and Cleaving

1. Thomas J. Stanley & William D. Danko, *The Millionaire Next Door* (Atlanta: Longstreet Press, 1996), 142.
2. Ibid., 165.
3. Ibid., 164–65.
4. Ibid., 29.

CHAPTER NINE — Wives in the Workforce

1. Larry Burkett, *Women Leaving the Workplace* (Chicago: Moody Press, 1995), 14.
2. Ibid., 41.

RESOURCES

BOOKS BY RON BLUE

Master Your Money

This best-selling book, revised for the nineties, explains the biblical principles of finance and stewardship combined with application in today's financial world.

Raising Money-Smart Kids

Based on the belief that parenting includes not only a huge financial investment but also the investment of spiritual wealth, this book teaches parents how to train their children to be good stewards.

Storm Shelter

Regardless of where the local, national, or global economy takes us, financial principles that succeeded thousands of years ago will continue to succeed tomorrow. No matter what your income level, no matter what your tolerance for investment risk, *Storm Shelter* shows you how to prepare for the future by building a financial strategy resting on the firmest of foundations.

Taming the Money Monster

This book teaches proper use of debt and how Christians can reduce or eliminate debt to accomplish God's purposes and achieve biblical stewardship.

ORGANIZATIONS

Sound Mind Investing

A monthly Christian financial journal published by Austin Pryor. This publication can serve as a resource for those individuals looking to learn more about biblical investing and how to manage their own portfolio. You can request information by writing SMI, P.O. Box 22128-R, Louisville, KY 40252-0128.

Christian Financial Concepts

Founded by Larry Burkett, this ministry serves as a resource for those looking to free themselves from the entanglement of debt. They have a number of materials as well as trained lay counselors available throughout the country. You can contact them at 800-722-1976.

Crown Ministries

Crown Ministries offers a small group study designed to reveal the scriptural plan for financial management and accountability. Well-suited to both couples and individuals, the study provides a practical message to develop a spending plan and make financial decisions. For information, call 888-972-7696 or visit their web site at www.crown.org.

ABOUT
RONALD BLUE AND CO.

Ronald Blue & Co. (RBC) was founded in 1979 and is a nationally recognized firm with fifteen branch offices. RBC offers fee-only financial planning services to help individuals achieve their short- and long-term goals. Planning services include

- Investment analysis
- Insurance analysis
- Retirement planning
- Estate planning
- Tax planning
- Charitable giving planning

If you are interested in receiving more information about Ronald Blue & Co. services, please write or call us at

Ronald Blue & Co.
Client Services
1100 Johnson Ferry Road
Suite 600
Atlanta, GA 30342
800-987-2987
www.ronblue.com
e-mail: clientservices@ronblue.com

Finding Contentment Through Giving

GENEROUS LIVING

Ron Blue
with Jodie Berndt

Financial advisor Ron Blue explains why an openhanded spirit is the key to freedom, contentment, and joy. In this book, he shows what happens when you become a giver, and helps you start right where you are, cultivating a generous lifestyle.

Pointing you beyond guilt-induced giving, Blue shows you the true, Bible-based way to give effectively, joyfully, and wisely.

You'll gain important insights into making a will, setting up a trust and foundation, and teaching your children to give. But better still, you'll find out:

- Why to give
- How to give
- Where is best to give
- When and how often to give

"An outstanding book, greatly needed . . . thoroughly biblical and wonderfully practical."

—HOWARD DAYTON, PRESIDENT, CROWN MINISTRIES

"Every ministry leader in America needs a case of these in his or her car."

—BRIAN KLUTH, PRESIDENT,
CHRISTIAN STEWARDSHIP ASSOCIATION

Softcover 0-310-21090-9

We want to hear from you. Please send your comments about this book
to us in care of the address below. Thank you.

ZondervanPublishingHouse
Grand Rapids, Michigan 49530
http://www.zondervan.com